OUTDOOR SURVIVAL & SUSTAINABILITY

ESSENTIAL WILDERNESS SKILLS FOR EMERGENCY PREPAREDNESS AND SELF-SUFFICIENCY

KNOWLEDGE CRAFTED BY NATURE, KAPENA MARINA

PRONOIA PUBLISHING LLC

CONTENTS

INTRODUCTION

Do you remember the days of childhood when a stick could be a sword, and the backyard was a vast kingdom? Well, who says the fun has to stop now that we've traded our capes for coats and our swords for smartphones? Welcome to the grown-up version of adventure—outdoor survival, where the stakes are real, and the rewards are countless. Whether you're looking to prep for unexpected city power outages or aiming to go full Caveman in the wilderness, I have written this guide to help and prepare you every step of the way.

Growing up in the heart of Texas, my childhood was endless adventures along riverbanks under wide-open skies. I was known as the "Barefoot Wild Child," a title worn like a badge of pride, and still holds to this day. The thrill of foraging for blackberries or learning which knots to use while tying together a raft wasn't just play; it was an early education in the rhythms of nature. While other kids might have been glued to screens, I was covered in mud, following the tracks of deer or watching with keen interest as sprouts emerged from our homemade compost. Those formative experiences deepened my connection with the environment and instilled a lasting passion, preparing me for *Outdoor Survival & Sustainability*.

The aim is not to scare you with the potential dangers of a disconnected world but to empower you with the skills to remain safe, self-sufficient, and resilient no matter your challenges. Preparedness isn't about fear but proactive engagement with the world. It's about ensuring that you can contribute positively to your community's resilience while finding personal fulfillment in the skills you develop.

My passion for the outdoors has continued to grow and become more practical over time. I spent a period of my life sailing across oceans, which provided numerous opportunities to perfect my knot-tying knowledge in high-stress situations, understand the predictability of weather, and gain invaluable experience in the world. Not to mention, living without refrigeration was a challenge that opened doors to the world of preservation like never before.

Recently, my journey took me to the beautiful isle of Maui. Hawaii. The tranquility of island life was abruptly interrupted by the devastating Lahaina fire. It was a stark reminder of how unprepared I was despite my knowledge. This event wasn't just a distant news story but a personal wake-up call about the importance of preparation and planning. In situations like these, being prepared isn't just about survival; it's about having the peace of mind to face whatever comes your way.

So, why am I sharing all of this? Because our experiences, especially the challenging ones, shape and prepare us for the unexpected. *Outdoor Survival and Sustainability* aren't just concepts—they're practical skills that can make a real difference in our lives. Whether you're a seasoned explorer or just starting your journey, remember that preparation is key. Learn, practice, be patient, and most importantly, enjoy the adventure.

So, let's get started. Step into your backyard, a nearby park, or the wilderness beyond. With every page turned, you'll be stepping closer to becoming a more capable, resourceful, and independent individual. This journey is about more than surviving—it's about being prepared, finding freedom, and reconnecting with the earth that sustains us all. Let's embark on this adventure together and rediscover the satisfaction of doing things with our hands.

CHAPTER ONE

PROPER PLANNING, PREPARATION, AND PRACTICALITY

W hether it's a howling hurricane, a terrifying tornado, or just a pesky power outage, life has a knack for throwing curveballs when we least expect it. This chapter isn't about wrapping you in a bubble of paranoia—far from it! Instead, think of it as your secret playbook for turning chaos into calm, ensuring that when Mother Nature decides to crash your party, you'll be the cool-headed host who has it all under control.

Creating a Personalized Survival Plan

Whether it's a howling hurricane, a terrifying tornado, or just a pesky power outage, life has a knack for throwing curveballs when we least expect it. This chapter isn't about wrapping you in a bubble of paranoia—far from it! Instead, think of it as your secret playbook for turning chaos into calm, ensuring that when Mother Nature decides to crash your party, you'll be the cool-headed host who has it all under control.

Developing Communication Strategies

We might rely too much on our smart devices in the digital age. Remembering phone numbers? That's so 1990s. However, when technology fails, having a physical list of essential contacts is as golden as that old mixtape you found in the attic. This list should include local emergency services, nearby hospitals, and a contact list of family members. Ensuring everyone in your household knows where this list is located can be as crucial as having it. Keep everything written in pencil. If the paper gets wet, the lead will not run, unlike ink from a pen.

Assigning Emergency Roles

It's all hands on deck in an emergency; everyone must know their role. Assigning specific responsibilities ensures that no critical tasks are overlooked. From who manages resources to assigning a chief communicator, even little Timmy can handle more than just the flashlight. Defining these roles beforehand avoids the "too many cooks in the kitchen" scenario. Tailor these roles to your household's strengths and capabilities.

Have you ever watched a fire drill become a confused parade of people unsure which way is up? That's exactly what we want to avoid. Regular drills transform your emergency plan from words on a page into a smooth action movie (minus Tom Cruise). Practice evacuating by different exits and even set up a temporary shelter. It might feel like a drill sergeant move, but these rehearsals could turn panic into purpose when push comes to shove.

Stress Management

When the winds howl louder than my mother-in-law at Thanksgiving dinner, and the walls shake like they've joined a dance competition, it's normal for your nerves to be as frayed as that old sweater you've meant to toss out. But here's the scoop: recognizing and managing stress amid chaos is like having a secret weapon tucked into your belt.

Stress is that sneaky thief who steals your peace of mind. It creeps up on you, masquerading as irritability—you're snapping at the dog, the TV, even your beloved coffee mug. Then there's fatigue, that heavy, all-encompassing tiredness that no amount of caffeine can combat. You might find yourself staring at your emergency plan but unable to focus, or suddenly, you're either ravenous or the thought of food makes you queasy.

Use simple techniques like deep breathing or visualization to maintain composure. For instance, the 5-5-7 breathing technique—inhaling for five seconds, holding for five seconds, and exhaling for seven seconds—can reset your body's stress response. Visualization exercises can mentally transport you to a peaceful setting, helping calm your mind amid chaos. Recognizing these signs early isn't just about self-awareness; it's about taking control when you feel you have little.

Psychological Resilience

Resilience is the incredible ability to recover from or adjust easily to misfortune or change. Picture it as your psychological immune system, built on adaptability, perseverance, and optimism. Cultivating these traits involves reframing challenges as growth opportunities, setting SMART goals, and practicing problem-solving under pressure.

Building resilience is like climbing a mountain—it takes determination, the right tools, and learning to navigate the rough patches. Setting realistic goals is a good starting point. These aren't your run-of-the-mill New Year's resolutions that are forgotten by February. These goals should be SMART:

Specific: Pin down exactly what needs to happen.

Measurable: Keep track of your wins, no matter how small.

Achievable: Set realistic and practical goals based on your resources and environment to avoid wasted energy or frustration.

Relevant: Your actions should tie directly to what is happening.

Time-bound: Work within a timeline that is reasonable to stay efficient.

Practicing problem-solving under stress is also crucial. The middle of a power outage is not the time to realize you can't find the flashlight. Regularly test yourself and your household with hypothetical scenarios. What would you do if the water supply was cut off? How would you communicate if cell phones stopped working? These mental fire drills prepare you to think clearly under pressure.

Reflection transforms past emergencies into future preparedness. Maintaining a resilience journal to analyze your responses to crises helps identify what worked and what didn't. This habit turns hindsight into foresight, allowing you to adapt and refine your strategies. Each experience becomes a stepping stone, equipping you with the knowledge to handle future challenges more confidently.

On-the-Go vs. Stay-and-Defend

Let's differentiate between your portable kit and your home kit. Your grab-and-dash survival pack should be lightweight, compact, and ready immediately. Your home kit can be more comprehensive, containing larger, more significant quantities of water, food, and supplies that cater to prolonged periods of self-sufficiency. Think comfortable and extensive with blankets, solar or hand crank chargers, a camping stove with extra fuel, and other resources to keep you safe and sound until the storm passes or help arrives.

Bug Out Bag- aka BOB

Remember those trips where you packed everything but the kitchen sink, convinced that you'd somehow need that third spare tire or a dozen extra socks? Well, crafting your lightweight Bug-Out-Bag is NOT like that. This time, every single article has to earn its keep. The key here is multipurpose items that pull double or triple duty. A brightly colored scarf that turns into a sling, visual aid, and water filter or a pot that doubles as a digging tool are just a few examples.

Every BOB starts with the essentials. Water is your number one priority. A good rule of thumb is one gallon per person daily, aiming for at least a 72-hour supply. A life-straw or portable filter is an excellent option where freshwater sources are accessible. Next up, food—non-perishable, easy-to-prepare items are your culinary VIPs here. Think of high-energy foods, like nuts and dried meat, and comfort snacks (because stress eating can totally be part of your survival strategy). Then, of course, there's a sturdy utility knife, reliable fire starter, flashlights, and extra batteries that should all be packed. First aid supplies must include bandages, antiseptics, prescribed medications, and pain relievers. And let's not forget about a good old-fashioned whistle and mirror—both are excellent tools when signaling for help, getting attention, or scarring away local wildlife. I have included my personal Bug-Out-Bag checklist at the end of this chapter.

Maintenance

An emergency kit isn't a "set it and forget it" type of deal. Check the expiry dates on all perishable items regularly—food, water, batteries, and medications all have shelf lives. And as your life changes—say, a new medical prescription or a growing child—your kit should adapt, too. Replace used or outdated supplies promptly; there's nothing more frustrating than reaching for a bandage only to find an empty box. Make it a quarterly event, a scavenger hunt to ensure everything is up-to-date and teach everyone about what's where in the process. Ensure each individual can carry their own pack.

Communication and Risks

Cell phones, while handy, often falter when disaster strikes due to overloaded networks or damaged infrastructure and can become about as useful as a chocolate teapot. That's where satellite phones and two-way radios come into the picture, offering a lifeline when traditional networks go belly-up. Satellite phones can be a game-changer, enabling calls to be made virtually anywhere on the planet, albeit often at a hefty cost and with the need for a clear shot at the sky.

Two-way radios (think walkie-talkies on steroids) are not just for kids or mall cops. These provide a more affordable and reliable option for local communication, making them ideal for coordinating with family or emergency teams within a few miles.

A battery-operated or hand-crank radio might seem like a relic from your grandpa's attic. Still, it can also be your best friend during a crisis. And yes, Amazon sells them in all colors, shapes, and sizes. Sign up for emergency alerts from local and national agencies to get notifications sent to your phone or radio; this will give you crucial minutes to act, whether to batten down the hatches or get the heck out of Dodge.

Incorporating Local Knowledge

Before you can fight the beast, you must know what you're up against. Every household's situation is as unique as a fingerprint. What's risky for a beachfront bungalow might be a non-issue for a downtown loft. Start by evaluating your area's environmental, geographical, and societal threats. Are you in Tornado Alley? Maybe industrial pollution or wildfire risks are more pertinent concerns where you live. Each scenario demands specific strategies and knowledge. Documenting these threats isn't just about having a list; it's about understanding the dynamics of these dangers so you can prepare effectively.

This knowledge is invaluable, from comprehending weather patterns to knowing the terrain. Take time to learn about the local climate changes and geographical features, as well as the flora and fauna of your specific region. Maybe even befriend a local expert or two; this isn't just book smarts—it's about being genuinely prepared.

Protecting Your Home During Natural Disasters

Fortifying your fortress is essential to withstand nature's wrath. Start with the basics: secure roof tiles, clear gutters to prevent water damage, and reinforce garage doors, often a structural weak point, to ensure they don't compromise your home's integrity.

Wildfires: From very personal experience, fire can move quickly, making preparation and foresight essential. Clear flammable vegetation around the property and trim trees. Use fire-resistant materials for roofing and siding to reduce risk. Install ember-resistant vents to prevent sparks from entering. Keep a long garden hose ready and consider external sprinklers. Be prepared to abandon ship; there's only so much you can do. Know and practice multiple escape routes, and I suggest putting a pair of bolt cutters in your vehicle.

Flooding: Waters can rise unexpectedly, so proactive measures are important. Seal basement walls with waterproofing materials and consider installing a sump pump with a backup power source to reduce seepage. Clear gutters, downspouts, and storm drains to direct water away from your home. Safeguard utilities by knowing how to shut off gas, water, and electricity, and do so early to prevent electrical fires or gas leaks. Elevate or waterproof major appliances like washers, dryers, and HVAC systems, or move them to higher levels. Install backflow valves to prevent sewage backup. Use sandbags or flood barriers at doors, windows, and garages to redirect water and seal cracks in your foundation.

Hurricanes and Tornadoes: High winds require strong defenses. Protect windows with storm shutters to block flying debris. Reinforce roofs with hurricane straps and bolt doors securely. Identify a windowless interior room, such as a walk-in closet or sturdy basement, as a safe space. If you live in a mobile home, plan for an alternate shelter. Stay vigilant and ready to act quickly if a warning is issued.

Earthquakes: Secure heavy items like bookshelves, mirrors, and TVs to walls and place heavier objects on lower shelves to prevent falling. Use latches on cabinets to keep contents from spilling. Identify safe spots in your home, such as under sturdy furniture or against interior walls, and practice "drop, cover, and hold on" drills. Know how to shut off utilities such as gas, water, and electricity to prevent fires or leaks after a quake. Keep fire extinguishers accessible and ensure everyone knows how to use them. If you live in a tsunami-prone area, identify evacuation routes and stay prepared to move to higher ground immediately after a quake.

Power Outages: These can create significant challenges and are the most likely to occur. A generator or solar panels with battery storage can keep essentials running. Insulate the home to maintain comfort during extreme weather. Keep battery-powered lanterns or LED lights readily available. To preserve food longer, keep the refrigerator and freezer doors closed as much as possible; a refrigerator stays cold for about four hours, and a full freezer for up to 48 hours if unopened. Before an outage, freeze water containers to use as ice packs, lower appliance temperatures, and group items to retain cold longer. During the blackout, monitor temperatures with thermometers, use coolers for frequently accessed items and consume or cook perishables early. Stock up on dry ice, ice packs, and non-perishables to stay prepared. If there is fear of the water also being shut off, fill the bathtub.

After the Crisis

Insurance is a cornerstone of preparedness. Ensure your coverage matches the regional risks you face, with sufficient limits to repair or rebuild your home if necessary. Maintaining an emergency fund is equally important; it provides a financial safety net for immediate needs or extended recovery periods. Having funds readily accessible can alleviate stress during uncertain times.

Recovery is not just physical but mental. Allow yourself and your family time to process the event, and seek support when needed. Recovery is a marathon, not a sprint, and every small step forward contributes to restoring normalcy.

Community Plans

Lastly, consider the power of the community. Setting up or joining a community communication plan can significantly enhance your chances of getting through a disaster unscathed. These plans involve coordinating with neighbors and local authorities to share information and resources, such as a generator. Imagine a neighborhood watch but for emergencies. Everyone keeps an eye out for each other and shares updates through whatever means, be it radio, online forums, or even a physical bulletin board at the local gathering spot.

Conclusion

Preparedness is about empowerment, not fear. You can confidently face life's challenges by embracing a proactive mindset, organizing survival essentials, and fostering resilience. Whether monitoring the weather, fortifying your home, or maintaining emergency plans, each step builds a foundation for safety and adaptability. Life's storms may be inevitable, but with preparation, you're ready for anything—even the occasional dragon.

Please go through and personalize the checklist provided on the following pages. It's recommended to create a notebook to consolidate information, such as addresses and phone numbers, and keep essential side notes on the refrigerator. Again, please keep this information written in pencil, as pen ink runs when it gets wet.

Bug Out Bag Checklist

Often called a BOB, is your lifeline. Think of it as a backpack filled with essential items that can sustain you for at least 72 hours when you must leave your home in a hurry. Here's a comprehensive list of items I encourage, plus a little more...

Regularly review and replace expired items. Update clothing, prescriptions, and adjust supplies based on seasonal changes. The internet recommends doing so quarterly.

Choose a durable, waterproof backpack or duffel bag with comfortable carrying straps. Everyone should be able to transport their own. If children are present, prepare yourself for the superpower of parenthood.

1. Water: Minimum 1 gallon (~4 liters) per person.

2. Food: Non-perishable, easy-to-prepare items like energy bars, canned goods, dehydrated fruits, meats, and meals. Don't forget your nuts!

3. First Aid Kit: Including bandages, antiseptic wipes, pain relievers, tweezers, a small magnifying glass, and any personal medications.

4. Multi-Tool or Knife: A versatile tool for various tasks. Think can opener, wine corks, and more. Keep the blade Sharp.

5. Emergency Blanket: Reflective type to retain body heat and can be used as a signaling device.

6. Fire Starter: Lighters, waterproof matches, flint, and steel—I recommend all three.

7. Flashlight or Headlamp: With spare batteries or a rechargeable option.

8. Whistle & Mirror: Signaling for help.

9. Navigation: Map, compass, and GPS device.

10. Personal Hygiene Items: Toothbrush, toothpaste, hand sanitizer, compostable toilet paper, menstrual products, etc.

11. Cash: There is no right or wrong amount, suggest smaller bills and a photocopy of the back and front of a current credit card.

12. Emergency Contact Information, Written in Pencil.

13. Change of Clothes: Including socks and underwear. With comfort and practicality in mind, bring as much as you want to carry.

14. Rain Gear: Poncho or waterproof jacket.

15. Sturdy Shoes or Boots: Comfortable for walking long distances.

16. Hat and Gloves: Protect from sun or cold.

17. Tarp or Tent: Lightweight for shelter. Walking sticks double as a tent pole.

18. Sleeping Bag or Blanket: Compact and appropriate for the climate.

Tools and Supplies:

19. Duct Tape: Useful for repairs and improvisations.

20. Paracord and Rope: Versatile for various uses. I'd recommend as much as you're willing to carry. Only cut when needed- always

make it a little longer than you think. Burn or tape ends immediately to keep from fraying.

21. Water Purification Tablets and Filter.

22. Radio: Battery-operated or hand-crank for emergency broadcasts.

23. Notepad and Pencil: For recording information and observations. Pencils ink doesn't run when wet.

24. Aluminum Foil, preferably "heavy- duty".

Personal and Miscellaneous Items:

25. Personal Documents and Hard Drive with Backups: Copies of ID, insurance papers, and important contacts. Keep waterproof.

26. Entertainment: Deck of cards, books, or other small items for morale.

27. Extra Batteries: For devices like flashlights or radios.

28. Fishing Gear: A handline and small collection of hooks for when near bodies of water.

29. Self-Defense Items: Depending on legality and personal preference (i.e., pepper spray or bear spray).

30. Spare Keys: Home, car, or other essential locks.

Additional Considerations:

31. Baby Supplies: Formula, diapers, wipes, if applicable.

32. Pet Supplies: Food, water, leash, if you have pets.

33. Local Maps: In case of GPS failure.

34. Seasonal Supplies: Depending on the climate and time of year.

Because We can Always Use More Things...

35. Sewing Kit: For repairs on clothing or gear.

36. Face Mask: For protection from smoke or dust.

37. Portable Solar Charger: For charging devices.

38. Camp Stove or Portable Cooking System: When you're not feeling full caveman.

Customize your Bug Out Bag based on location, climate, personal health needs, and any unique considerations. Ensure everyone in your household has their own BOB tailored to them.

CHAPTER TWO

SAVVY STRATEGIES FOR SUCCESSFUL OFF-GRID SURVIVAL

S o, you've decided to embrace the wild, or perhaps the wild has chosen you. This chapter is your essential companion, equipping you with the fundamental survival skills necessary to thrive, from mastering the art of purifying water to igniting fire and constructing shelters. These skills ensure your safety and comfort and deepen your connection with nature, fostering resilience and self-reliance in the face of the unknown.

Water Purification Techniques

In the grand theater of survival skills, water purification takes center stage. Let's just say it deserves a standing ovation. Imagine you're deep in the woods, surrounded by the silence you can't find in any city. Beautiful, yes, but also a bit daunting, especially when you're thirsty, and the only water in sight is the kind you wouldn't normally consider drinking. That's where mastering the fine art of water purification adds comfort and becomes essential for survival.

Understanding the Source

First off, not all water is created equal. The idyllic stream bubbling might look like the perfect place to fill your bottle, but slow your roll there, partner. Surface water can be teeming with pathogens and pollutants, depending on its source and what's upstream. Start by scouting for flowing water versus stagnant pools, as moving water is less likely to harbor bacteria and parasites. However, don't be fooled—this water still needs treatment. If you're in a mountainous area, springs can be a gold mine of fresh water, typically cleaner due to natural filtration through the earth. But remember, treating it is a must, no matter how pristine the water looks.

Boiling Water

Let's start with the old reliable: water boiling. It's like the superhero of water purification methods—simple, effective, and powerful. Boiling is king because it zaps most pathogens in the water, making it safe to drink. But here's the catch: it's not just about bringing water to a boil; it's about keeping it there long enough to do its job.

As you go higher in altitude, the air pressure drops, which means water boils at a lower temperature. So, at **sea level**, water boils at 100°C (212°F), which is hot enough to kill most pathogens in just a minute or two. But at **5,000 feet**, water boils at around 95°C (203°F), and by the time you're at **10,000 feet**, it's closer to 90°C (194°F).

Even though it boils quicker at high altitudes, it's not as hot, so it takes a bit longer to purify. My rule of thumb is to boil water for at least **3 minutes** if you're above **6,500 feet**. Better safe than sorry, remember that patience isn't just a virtue but a necessity.

Solar Water Disinfection (SODIS)

For those sunny days, SODIS is like having a free water purifier. You need a clear plastic bottle (sorry, no fancy colored glass here) and Mr. Sunshine. Fill the bottle, cap it, give a good shake to oxygenate, and place it to catch full sunlight for 6 hours. The UV rays will handle the rest, neutralizing harmful pathogens. Make sure the bottles aren't bigger than a liter for optimal UV penetration, and if the water is murky, filter it through a cloth first. It's eco-friendly, cost-effective, and a brilliant way to purify water using just the basics.

DIY Water Filters

Ever feel like crafting something that's both fun and lifesaving? Then, making a water filter is a go-to project, especially if kids are around. You'll need charcoal, sand, and stones or gravel. Layer gravel at the bottom, then sand and charcoal on top in a container, like a bottle with the bottom cut off. Pour your dubious water in, and let gravity pull it through this natural filtration system, trapping contaminants. It's not perfect, though it's a significant improvement from what you started with, so boiling or disinfecting after filtration is wise.

Chemical Purification

For those who skipped chemistry class to doodle in notebooks, here's a practical application: chemical purification. This is where iodine and chlorine drops shine. Think of them as your water's personal bodyguards, kicking out harmful bacteria and viruses on the spot. Iodine is great because it's lightweight and easy to carry. Still, it can leave a funny taste in your mouth and isn't suitable for pregnant women or those with thyroid conditions. Chlorine is friendlier on the palate and can also be used safely by most people. Just a few drops, a bit of patience while the chemicals do their dance, and voila—safer water. However, remember that these chemicals aren't effective against all contaminants, like certain protozoa, so always consider the water source. And always follow the package instructions to the letter, because when it comes to chemical purifiers, more isn't merrier.

Filter Systems and Natural Filtration Methods

Portable water filters and straws are like having a water treatment plant in your pocket. They're designed for on-the-go use, filtering out pathogens and, in some cases, chemicals too. Maintenance is key—regular cleaning and filter replacement (according to manufacturer guidelines) ensure these gadgets keep doing their job effectively.

Storing Purified Water

Once you've secured and purified your water, the next hurdle is to store it safely. Use clean containers, preferably ones designed for water storage, and keep them sealed and out of direct sunlight. Contamination post-purification is a real bummer and can undo all your hard work. Think of it as safeguarding your liquid treasure—after all, in the wild, good water isn't just nice to have; it's your lifeline.

There you have it, a primer on mastering the art of finding water in the wild. Whether you're boiling, filtering, or disinfecting with the sun's rays, each method has its place in your survival toolkit. And remember, staying hydrated isn't just about drinking water; it's about ensuring its safety.

Fire-Building and Protection

Imagine you're out in the wild, the air is crisp, and all you need to complete that perfect outdoor tableau is a warm, welcoming fire. But here's the twist—no lighters, no matches, just you, nature, and some old-school know-how. Let's start with the fire triangle basics: heat, fuel, and oxygen. These three musketeers of combustion must be perfectly balanced to get your fire roaring.

Prepare the Materials

Choosing the right kind of fuel is your first step; this isn't the place for those big, chunky logs yet. It would be best to have the small stuff—dry leaves, grass, pine needles, or my favorite, birch bark, which catches fire faster than gossip spreads at a family reunion. Think small, dry twigs or split wood pieces no thicker than a pencil for kindling. These will catch fire from your tinder and help build enough heat to ignite the larger fuel wood, which brings us to choosing the right fuel. Opt for seasoned wood, which sounds like something you'd find in a chef's kitchen, but really, it's just wood that's been dried for at least six months. Wet or green wood is a no-go; it'll smoke like it's trying to signal aliens rather than provide a warm blaze.

Lay a base of tinder in the center of the fire ring. Ensure it's dry and fluffy to catch the flame quickly. Arrange the kindling sticks around the tinder in a teepee shape, leaving enough space for air to flow. Use an ember or char cloth (a small piece of fabric made from natural material that's been charred but not burned) to ignite the tinder. Gently blow on the base of the fire to provide oxygen, helping the tinder and kindling to ignite fully. Once the kindling is burning well, gradually add larger pieces of fuel wood. Place them in a way that allows air to circulate through the fire. Continue to feed the fire with fuel as needed. Adjust the placement of the wood to ensure a steady burn.

Friction-Based Fire Making

For the magic of making fire through sheer willpower and friction, have you ever tried rubbing your hands together on a cold day to warm up? Now imagine doing that with wood; voila, you've got the hand drill method. First up, choose your wood. You want the spindle and the fireboard to be made of softwood, as it generates enough friction but is easy to work with. Good choices include cedar, spruce, or poplar.

The shape of your spindle should be a sturdy, dry wood, five to eight inches long and about the width of your thumb. One end should be bluntly pointed. For the fireboard, aim for half an inch thick and flat. Using the point of a knife or a sharp rock, create a small divot in the fireboard. Start near one end of the board; you will move along the length of the board, making several holes as you start more fires. The divot should be about an inch or so from the edge, depending on the width of your spindle.

When you're ready, place the spindle's pointed side into the divot and twirl it rapidly between your palms, pressing down gently. It's a real workout, and it might make you feel like you're auditioning for a role as a cave dweller, but the reward is a glowing ember.

Bow Drill Method

If the hand drill sounds too primitive, upgrade to the bow drill method. It's like the CrossFit workout of fire starting. You'll take your spindle- now sharpened at both ends- and fireboard from above, but now use a bow to spin the spindle, which is easier on the hands and more efficient. The setup now includes a bow, a spindle, a fireboard, and a bearing block (a piece of wood, stone, or shell used to hold the top of the spindle in place). It's a setup, but you'll feel like a fire-making wizard once you get the hang of it.

Now, posture is critical here. Sit comfortably on the ground, place the fireboard on a stable surface, and hold it steady with your foot. With a sturdy yet flexible curve, the bow should be about as long as your arm from shoulder to fingertips. Attach a strong cord, or shoelace, to either end of the bow, leaving it slack enough to wrap around the spindle but tight enough to hold it firmly in place. Use one hand to hold the top of the spindle (use a socket like a stone or wood piece to protect your hand) and twist the spindle into the cord with the other. The loop will grasp the spindle, and you will be able to saw the bow back and forth smoothly. Place the blunt end of the spindle into the depression in the fireboard. Grip the bow with your dominant hand and begin sawing back and forth. The spindle should spin rapidly. Apply steady, downward pressure on the spindle with the handhold while maintaining a smooth, even sawing motion.

It's a marathon, not a sprint. Keep a steady pace, apply consistent pressure, and soon you'll have smoke, and then an ember. Carefully transfer this ember to a nest of tinder, blow gently, and watch as your fire lights up like the stage at a rock concert, except the pyrotechnics are all natural.

Flint and Steel Techniques

When it comes to sparking up a fire with flint and steel selecting your flint and steel is crucial. You want a piece of flint sharp enough to shave off tiny splinters of steel when struck. These tiny splinters must be hot enough to glow and ignite your tinder. Now, the striking technique isn't just whacking them together willy-nilly. You need a swift, downward strike at an angle that maximizes the contact, creating those precious sparks. Imagine you're slicing a piece of cake with an extra sharp knife—that kind of precision and finesse. Hold the steel above your tinder and strike downwards against the flint, aiming to direct sparks into your tinder pile. It's a skill that might take a few tries to perfect, but once you've got it, you got it. Just remember, practice makes perfect.

Fire from Ice: Natures Magnifyn Glass

If you find yourself with plenty of ice but no clear fire-making tools, don't panic. Under the right conditions, ice can be a surprisingly effective tool for starting a fire. The trick here is to shape the ice into a lens, much like the magnifying glass you used to fry ants with as a kid. First, find clear ice—transparency is vital as opaque ice (like that frosty stuff from your freezer) which won't focus the sunlight. Shape the ice using your hands, gloves, or even a knife into a smooth, convex lens around the size of a small plate. The shaping process might require some melting and refreezing to achieve clarity, so patience is a virtue here. Once shaped, angle your ice lens towards the sun, directing the focused rays onto your tinder like any other magnifying lens. It might take a few tries to find the perfect angle and distance, but with persistence, those rays will heat your tinder enough to catch fire. It's a method that gets you fire and earn some serious bragging rights.

Utilizing Random Objects

Now, let's think outside the box—or the fire ring, so to speak. Nature's filled with tools and materials that can kickstart a fire. If you know where to look, do you have a clear plastic bottle or a bag of water? Use it as a lens to focus sunlight onto your tinder, just like those naughty days when using a magnifying glass to zap bugs. Or how about steel wool? Yep, that stuff under your kitchen sink. Connect it to the terminals of a battery, and it'll glow red-hot in seconds. Just be sure to have your tinder ready because it's a fleeting moment of fiery glory.

Maintaining and Transporting Fire

Congratulations, you got fire, but keeping it alive and protecting your flame from wind and rain is paramount. Building a wind-break or setting up your fire under a natural shelter can shield those precious flames. But what about when you need to move? Transporting fire was a vital skill for ancient nomads and could be for you, too. One method is to create a fire bundle or ember carrier; this can be as simple as a can or piece of bark folded into a container. Place hot embers into your carrier, surrounded by some fuel material that's not too quick to burn, like partially charred wood. If you're moving short distances, this ember carrier can keep your fire alive for hours. Remember, safety comes first—ensure your carrier is sturdy and you're not at risk of dropping hot embers as you trek.

Mastering these fire-making skills offers more than warmth and bragging rights; it deepens your connection to the ancient human art of fire mastery. It refers to a time when fire meant survival, sto-rytelling, and community. So whether you're sparking a flame with flint and steel or laboriously spinning a bow drill, it's a reminder of the resourcefulness and resilience within us, waiting to be ignited. Next time you're out in the wild, or even in your backyard, take a moment to try these techniques. Feel the warmth of the fire, watch the flames dance, and know that you've tapped into something elemental and profoundly human.

Using Fire for Signaling and Protection

Let's turn the heat up a notch and discuss how fire isn't just for cozy campfire stories or roasting those marshmallows to golden perfection—it's also a critical survival tool. Picture this: you're lost, it's getting dark, and you need to signal for help. Or maybe you're just trying to keep some overly curious wildlife at bay. Either way, mastering fire for signaling and protection is like having an insurance policy that pays out in safety and peace of mind.

Fire for Signaling Rescue

So you're a castaway, maybe complete with the ocean and volleyball companion. You need to get the attention of rescuers, and what better way to shout "Here I am!" than with a plume of smoke? But not just any smoke. You need thick, billowing white smoke that screams for attention. Here's how you do it: gather green vegetation—leaves, branches, anything still full of moisture. Once you have a decent fire going, throw this greenery on top. It'll generate a lot of smoke! Positioning your fire is also vital. You want a clearing where the smoke can rise freely, visible against the skyline day and night.

Protective Fires

Now, let's switch gears to keep those critters at bay. Fire can be your shield, whether it's a curious bear or just mosquitoes that think you're an all-you-can-eat buffet. The trick? It's all about the materials you burn. Some woods, like birch or pine, have oils that can help repel insects and even larger animals. And let's not forget our smoky friend from the signaling fires—smoke is a great deterrent. To set up a protective perimeter, build small fires around your campsite, using stones to create a barrier that keeps the fire contained. Keep fires at a manageable size and always attended. It's about creating a barrier, not a bonfire dance party.

Emergency Heat Source

Moving on to warmth—because, let's face it, few things are as miserable as being cold. Creating a fire that efficiently radiates heat can turn a freezing night into a toasty outdoor experience. The reflector fire is your best friend here. Set up your fire against a backdrop of rocks or build a wall of earth behind it. This setup protects the fire from wind and reflects the heat back towards you, turning your campsite into a cozy haven. It's like having a natural heater that provides light and protection. The layout of your fire is crucial; think of it as arranging furniture in your living room for the best TV view. Only, instead of binging the latest season of your favorite show, you're catching waves of comforting warmth.

Fire Safety Practices

Last but certainly not least, let's talk about safety because there's no use in a good fire if it burns more than planned. Choosing the right location is step one. Avoid dry areas prone to wildfires and keep a clear space free of too much dry vegetation. Creating firebreaks, like trenches or cleared paths, can prevent a fire from spreading unintentionally. And when it's time to say goodnight, make sure your fire is out. Douse it with water, stir the ashes, and douse it again. Feel the ashes with the back of your hand to ensure no lingering heat.

Using fire responsibly and effectively in the wild opens up a world of safety and possibilities. From signaling rescues to fending off the night's chill, it's a tool that calls for respect and knowledge. So, whether you're lighting up the night for safety or gathering around for a heartwarming campfire tale, remember these tips. When used wisely, fire isn't just a survival element; it's a companion that lights up the dark, wards off the cold and keeps the wild at bay.

Shelters: Location and Building Strategies

When you're out embracing the wild, picking the perfect spot for your shelter is like choosing the best seat at a concert. You want a prime spot that enhances your experience and keeps you comfy, no matter what Mother Nature belts out. So, when scouting for your outdoor home-away-from-home, remember a few things. First, water proximity is crucial. Being near a water source saves you from long hikes to hydrate, but too close, you might find your sleeping bag turning into a waterbed if it rains. Land stability is another biggie. Avoid setting up camp on steep slopes or loose soil unless you fancy a midnight slide down the hill. Flat, stable ground is your friend here. Also, take a good look around and above for dead branches or shaky trees ready to crash down, literally. And, of course, consider exposure to the elements. A spot shielded by natural barriers like bushes or rock formations can offer sanctuary from winds and provide some natural insulation.

Materials

The real trick is in gathering the right components, which, thankfully, nature has in abundance. You're looking for sturdy branches, broad leaves, resilient grasses, and that primeval goo—mud. Each of these materials has its superpowers. Branches and logs are the bones of your shelter; they give it structure and strength. Aside from making a stylish natural roof, leaves and grass provide excellent insulation and waterproofing—crucial for those unexpectedly soggy nights. And mud? It's not just for spa treatments; it's a fantastic natural cement, perfect for filling in the gaps and keeping the wind at bay.

But not all branches are created equal, and here's where a bit of botanical know-how comes in handy. You want strong but somewhat flexible branches—think young saplings or resilient woods like hazel or willow. Leaves should be broad and preferably waxy, which helps them shed water like a duck's back. Grasses must be long and tough—great for weaving into mats or thatching. As for mud, look for a clay-rich mix, which is more likely to hold together and not just crumble away like a poorly made sandcastle.

Lean-To

It is like the studio apartment of wilderness accommodations – compact, efficient, and just enough to keep you dry and cozy. Start by finding two trees about a body's length apart. These are your main supports. Then, grab a long, sturdy branch and secure it horizontally between the two trees at about waist height; this is your ridgepole, the backbone of your lean-to. Next, lean some smaller branches against the ridgepole, creating a slanted wall. Angle them well enough to shed rain but not so steep that you sacrifice covered space. Layer foliage, like leaves or pine boughs, starting from the bottom and overlapping as you go up, like nature's shingles, not only keeps water out but also traps air, which is your invisible blanket of warmth. If you're feeling extra crafty, add a layer of bark for added waterproofing.

Debris Hut

Start with a sturdy ridgepole, one end on the ground, the other supported by a forked branch or wedged between two close-standing trees. Create a skeleton by placing branches along the length of the ridgepole, then pile on leaves, grass, or whatever you can get your hands on. The thicker, the better. Your goal is a dense pile that would take a serious poke to see daylight through. If snow is all you've got, it's time to channel your inner igloo builder. Compact the snow as you pile it up; it's surprisingly insulating and windproof. Line the floor with more insulating materials – dry leaves, ferns, or even your spare clothes. The result? A snug, well-insulated hideout that retains heat and shields you from the elements.

Complimentary

And then there are those times when Mother Nature provides a ready-made shelter. Caves and rock overhangs can be a real boon, offering natural protection with minimal effort. But proceed with caution. First, ensure the structure is sound—no loose rocks or risky overhangs. Check for signs of current animal residents; you don't want to bunk with a bear. Enhance what nature offers by blocking prevailing winds with a tarp or more branches. A fire at the cave's mouth can serve as both a beacon and a barrier, warming you up while deterring unwelcome wildlife. Remember, the key to using these natural shelters is to leave them as you found them. Your stay is temporary, but the impacts of your visit can be long-lasting.

Maintaining Shelter Safety

Building the shelter is just the beginning. Keeping it safe is where the real challenge lies. Regularly check for potential hazards—loose branches ready to fall, water build-up that could lead to a collapse, or even critters that might have decided your shelter is their new hangout spot. Ventilation is another crucial factor, especially if using a small, enclosed space. The last thing you want is to wake up feeling like you've just run a marathon in your sleep because of poor air circulation. Keep one side of the shelter open or ensure an air gap to let moisture out and fresh air in. Maintaining your shelter might not be glamorous, but it's essential for turning a temporary home in the wild into a safe haven rather than just some sticks thrown together.

The type of shelter you build can be as varied as the landscape you're in. Constructing with natural materials doesn't mean you should go full lumberjack on the nearest tree. The key is to use dead or fallen wood rather than cutting live branches, which helps preserve the health of the forest. Whether you construct a lean-to that faces the sunrise, a debris hut that blends into the forest, or utilize the ancient embrace of a cave, each shelter tells a story: A story of a night spent under the stars, of the whisper of the trees, or the call of the wild. So, choose your site carefully, build with respect, and rest easy, knowing you've woven a little bit of yourself into the tapestry of the wild.

Conclusion

Making mud shelters, crafting a fire bow, or jazzing up water with a pinch of iodine might seem like skills reserved for the intrepid explorer, but they're also incredibly empowering for anyone who wants to connect deeper with nature and ensure their hydration is safe, no matter where their adventures might take them. So, the next time you dip your toe into a mountain stream or scoop up a handful of lake water, remember these techniques. They're not just survival skills; they're your ticket to safer, more confident adventures in the great outdoors.

CHAPTER THREE

WILDERNESS WISDOM FOR WORRY-FREE WANDERING

I magine reading the weather like a seasoned sailor, deciphering the subtle shifts in wind and sky that hint at what's to come, or navigating through dense forests or vast plains, guided not only by a compass but also by the timeless wisdom of the stars glittering overhead. And then there are the knots—the intricate weavings of rope that transform simple lines into lifelines, securing tents, boats, and our very safety in the wild. In this article, we'll delve deeper into these essential skills that connect us with nature's rhythms and empower us to explore confidently and reverently. We'll start with weather prediction, move on to navigation, and finish with knot tying, each section building on the previous one to give you a comprehensive understanding of these essential outdoor skills.

Weather Prediction: Reading Signs in Nature

Have you ever wondered how our ancestors managed without the Weather Channel or those handy smartphone apps? It turns out that the natural world is brimming with hints about the weather if you know where to look. From cloud formations to animal behaviors, nature provides a free forecast to those who understand its signs. So, let's turn off the tech and tune into nature's network.

Cloud Interpretation

Clouds are nature's way of painting the sky, and they're not just there for their good looks—they tell stories about the weather. Reading these fluffy formations can let you know what's coming, weather-wise. Cumulus clouds, those puffy, cotton-like clouds that look like floating cotton candies, generally mean good weather. Watch them, though; if they start towering upward in the early afternoon, they might just grow up to become thunderstorms. On the other hand, cirrus clouds, those high, wispy clouds that streak across the sky, are made of ice and often indicate that a change in the weather is likely within the next 24 hours. And then there's the stratus cloud, which covers the sky like a gray blanket. When you see these, it's a good bet that drizzle or light rain is coming. It's like decoding a message from Mother Nature, giving you a heads-up to pack that raincoat or plan a cozy indoor day.

Animal Behavior

Animals, too, are keen observers of weather changes. Have you ever noticed birds flying lower than usual? That could mean bad weather is coming. Birds fly lower to avoid the discomfort of the lower air pressure that comes with a storm. Cows are also known to give us weather clues. They might be anticipating rain if you see them gathering closely together in a field. And let's remember our six-legged friends, the ants. They build their mounds with higher walls when they sense increased humidity and potential rain—nature's little engineers preparing for a storm. Observing these behaviors can give you a more intimate understanding of the environment and help you predict the weather with surprising accuracy. It's a reminder that humans aren't the only creatures that adjust their behavior based on the weather—animals have been expert meteorologists for centuries!

Wind Patterns and Pressure

Now, let's feel the wind and sniff the air—yes, really. Wind direction can tell you a lot about what type of weather to expect. Shifting wind direction to the south can bring warmer and wetter conditions in many areas. In contrast, a northern wind might suggest cooler, drier weather is on the way. And then there's the feel of the air. A sudden drop in air pressure, which can make your ears pop, often precedes a storm. This pressure drop can also cause a feeling of heaviness in the air. It might even bring a more profound, pungent odor from the forest as gasses from decomposing plant material are released—a sign to batten down the hatches.

Natural Barometers

Did you know that some plants can act as natural barometers? Take the humble pine cone, for example. Pine cones open up when the air is dry because their scales curl back. When it's going to rain, they close up to protect their seeds from water. Flowers, too, can tell us something about the weather. Many flowers open in sunny conditions and close up when rain is coming. Observing these subtle plant behaviors can provide valuable clues about the weather, enhancing your ability to prepare and respond to different conditions.

By paying attention to the sky, the behavior of animals, the direction of the wind, and the reactions of plants, you can become quite proficient at predicting the weather. This knowledge deepens your connection to the natural world and enhances your experience while in the wilderness. It reminds us that nature is interconnected, with each element—from the smallest ant to the highest cloud—playing a part in the larger ecosystem. So, the next time you step outside, take a moment to observe. The sky, the animals, and the plants are all part of nature's forecasting system, ready to share their secrets with those willing to learn.

Navigation: Compass and Natural Landmarks

Venturing into the wilderness offers a sense of freedom and adventure that few experiences can match. However, mastering the art of navigation is essential to enjoying the journey and ensuring your safety. This section will explore fundamental techniques: reading a compass, using natural landmarks, and celestial navigation. Each method helps you find your way and deepens your connection to the natural world. Imagine standing at the edge of a vast forest, feeling the magnetic pull of your compass, recognizing a familiar mountain peak, or charting your course by the stars. These skills turn every hike into a journey of discovery, allowing you to traverse landscapes with confidence and a sense of wonder.

Reading a Compass

Navigating with a compass isn't just for pirates or treasure hunters; it's a fundamental skill that is easy to do. Hold the compass flat in your hand or on a level surface. The needle will swing around – that's normal. It's just doing its dance before it points toward the magnetic north, which is a tad different from true north (that's the North Pole). Why does this matter? Because when you're trying to follow a map, aligning to true north keeps you on the right path. Now remember, the red end of the needle points north - a simple yet crucial detail that's easy to overlook in the thrill of an adventure.

Taking bearings is just the next step—figuring out the direction from one point to another. It's like drawing an invisible line straight from your feet to where you want to go, with the compass as your guide.

Identifying Natural Landmarks

Navigating by landmarks is another trusty technique. This can be anything noticeable – a peculiarly shaped tree, a mountain peak, or an artificial structure. The trick here is to use these landmarks in conjunction with the direction you're traveling. Say you're walking towards a mountain; keep it in front of you, and it becomes a guidepost. If you're returning, it should be behind you. It sounds simple, but in the maze of nature, a constant visual reference is invaluable, keeping you on track and preventing you from walking in circles, literally.

Sun and Stars for Direction

But what if your compass fell out of your pocket or got left behind? Before you panic, remember the sky is your oldest map. The sun always rises in the east and sets in the west, right? With this reliable celestial routine, you can figure out the cardinal points. During the day, stick a straight stick vertically into the ground (no leaning towers, please) and mark the tip of the shadow it casts. This mark is your west. Wait about 15 minutes, mark the new position of the shadow tip, and connect the two marks. This line runs approximately east-west, with the first mark being west. You've just used the oldest trick to find your way!

Now, let's chat about how the sun can tell time because, let's face it, a watch only works if you remember to charge it or wind it. The shadow stick method isn't just suitable for directions; it's also a primitive sundial. The shadow moves as the sun travels through the sky, shortest at noon and longer as the sun rises and sets. By observing the movement of the shadow, you can estimate the time of day, which can be crucial for planning your activities or knowing how much daylight you have left to find that perfect campsite or get back to civilization.

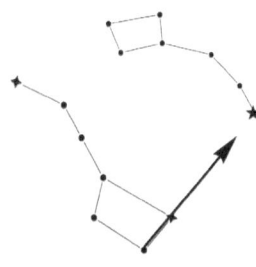

p.s. Polaris is Not the Brightest Star

Night falls, and it's a new world—a quieter, darker world where the stars come out to play. And play they do, in patterns that have guided sailors, explorers, and lost hikers for centuries. Learning key constellations can turn the night sky into your GPS. To locate Polaris, start by finding the Big Dipper (Ursa Major), one of the most recognizable constellations in the Northern sky. The two stars that form the outer edge of the Big Dipper's bowl are called the "pointer stars" because they point directly toward Polaris. Imagine drawing a line straight through these two stars—follow that line about five times the distance between them, and you'll land on Polaris.

Unlike other stars, Polaris doesn't rise or set. It remains almost fixed in the same spot in the sky because it's aligned with Earth's rotational axis. As a result, once you've found it, you'll know precisely where true north is.

For our Southern Hemisphere brothers and sisters, or if you happened to get lost 'Down Under,' look for Crux (the Southern Cross). It's a small, cross-shaped constellation. Extend an imaginary line down from its long axis. Then, find Alpha Centauri and Beta Centauri, the two bright stars nearby. Draw a perpendicular line from the middle of these two stars, and where the lines meet, point south.

The beauty of it is that the stars are always there, steady and unchanging, no matter where you are. Even without a compass or GPS, the sky offers natural navigation tools. It's like having an old, reliable friend watching over you on those nights, guiding you home. It may take a bit of practice, but once you learn to read the stars, you'll always have that sense of direction. The sky's got your back—trust it!

Creating Personal Markers and Mental Maps

As you trek through the wilderness, consider setting up personal markers, especially if you're venturing off the beaten path. These could be stacked stones, tied branches, or even a piece of fabric tied to a tree—anything that can help you identify your route when you return. Just ensure these markers are environmentally friendly and temporary. No one likes a litterbug, and in nature, it's critical to maintain the leave-no-trace principles. These markers are like leaving yourself a trail of digital breadcrumbs, except they're real.

Lastly, let's talk about mental maps. These are not just maps, but your personal, internal Google Maps. Creating mental maps involves paying close attention to your surroundings and noting details that can help orient you. It starts with observation—what's around you, how does the trail turn, where does the sun set, and what landmarks stand out? As you move, keep updating this mental map, and be sure to look around and do a 180 every so often. It's like drawing in your mind, where each memory is a stroke on the canvas. This map grows with every step, informed by the environment and your senses, helping you know where you are and find your way back or onward.

Navigating without modern tools is an art form that connects more deeply with the environment. It requires attention, memory, and a bit of creativity. But more than that, it instills a profound sense of place and direction that GPS screens can never quite capture. Each tool and technique offers a different way to engage with the wilderness, and by mastering these skills, you equip yourself to face the challenges of the wild with confidence and safety. So next time you step into the wilderness, take a moment to observe, listen, and orient yourself using these age-old methods. You'll find that the world speaks to those who know how to listen and that every landscape, whether bathed in sunlight or starlight, has paths waiting to be discovered.

Knot Tying and Practical Uses

Knots, my friends, are the unsung heroes of the survival world. Choosing the right knot for the right task can be as crucial as selecting the right gear. Each knot has its specialty and misusing them can be like using a butter knife to cut steak—frustrating and ineffective. Let's master some of the most practical, such as the square knot, figure-eight knot, and bowline.

Square Knot

Also known as a reef knot, it is helpful in various situations where you must join two ropes of the same diameter. It is excellent for latching bundles, securing items onto your backpack, and even in first aid for tying bandages and slings. However, avoid using a square knot for critical or heavy loads, as it can slip under pressure.

1. Hold the Ends: Take one rope in each hand.

2. Make an Overhand Knot:

    ○ Cross the right end over the left.

    ○ Now, tuck that right end under the left rope and pull tight.

3. Take an end in each hand:

- ○ Cross the left end over the right.

- ○ Now, tuck the left end under the right rope and pull tight.

The result should have both ends on the same side, and the knot should look symmetrical.

Figure Eight

Is versatile, reliable and commonly used in climbing, boating, and rescue operations. This knot is handy as a stopper to prevent the rope from slipping through a retaining device or pulley. While the figure eight knot is versatile and reliable, there are better choices for heavy loads, as it can be difficult to untie after being subjected to significant tension.

1. Hold the End of the Rope

2. Form a Loop:

- ○ Cross the working part— the end of the rope that you are actively manipulating.

- ○ Over the standing part— the longer, inactive portion of the rope that extends away and is typically held stationary.

3. Wrap Around:

- ○ Take the working end and wrap it around the standing part.

- ○ Pass the working end through the loop from behind.

4. Tighten:

  ○ Pull both ends to tighten the knot.

  ○ It should resemble the number eight.

Bowline

Best in situations when a secure, non-slip loop is needed. In climbing, the bowline is favored for tying into harnesses or creating
anchor points because it remains secure under load but is still easy
to untie afterward. In the wild, it's useful for setting up tents and
securing tarps. The main reason not to use a bowline is it can
un-knot under dynamic loads that lose and gain tension repeti-
tively or with very slippery ropes.

1. Make a Loop:

  ○ Form a small loop near the end of the
    rope.

  ○ Ensure the working end is on top of the
    standing part.

2. Pass the Working End:

  ○ Take the working end and pass it up through the loop
    from underneath.

3. Go Around the Standing Part:

  ○ Wrap the working end around the standing part of the
    rope.

4. Return to the Loop:

○ Pass the working end back down through the loop you
initially made.

5. Tighten the Knot:

○ Hold the working end and pull on the standing part to
tighten the knot.

○ Adjust as needed to ensure the loop is the desired size.

If this one seems trickier, you must channel your inner rabbit.
Picture the end of your rope as Bugs Bunny. He then comes up the
hole (the loop you made), goes around the tree (the rope's standing
part), and then back down the hole. "What's up, Doc?"

Practical Applications in Survival Situations

Now, imagining our ropes and knots in action, let's explore some
real-time applications. Constructing a raft? Those square lashing
will ensure your logs stay snugly together as you float downriver. If
you must evacuate an injured buddy, a series of bowline knots can
create a secure stretcher. These knots aren't just practical; they're
potentially lifesaving, turning a simple rope into the Swiss Army
knife of survival gear. It's about being prepared, versatile, and
ready to tackle challenges head-on with nothing but a rope and
some well-chosen knots.

Maintenance and Safety Checks

Maintaining your rope and ensuring your knots are in top shape
is as crucial as knowing how to tie them. Regularly inspect your
ropes for frays, snags, or weak spots. A compromised rope can
mean the difference between safety and disaster. Practice tying your knots until you can do them blindfolded (figuratively,
please—safety first!). Before you rely on a knot in a survival situ-

ation, test it under controlled conditions. Pull it, weigh it down, and check it from all angles. Make sure it's dressed neatly and set securely. Doing so isn't about being obsessive but ensuring reliability when needed. Your life and your companions' lives might hang on the integrity of a knot. So treat your ropes and knots with respect—they're the threads that bind your survival story together.

In this world, knowing how to use and manage your knots effectively is like having a superpower. It's about transforming simple strands into lifelines, shelters, and tools. And from personal experience, it's no fun to climb into a freshly hung hammock and end up on the ground with the wind knocked out of you. As we continue exploring the depths of survival skills, remember that each knot you tie and each loop you secure brings you closer to being a survivor and a master in the wild.

Conclusion

Mastering survival skills integrates a deep understanding of nature's cues and practical techniques. Tying knots isn't just about securing gear; it's a fundamental skill that ensures safety and efficiency in the wild. Celestial navigation taps into ancient wisdom, guiding travelers using the constellations and the North Star amidst the vastness of the night sky. Reading nature's clues involves observing cloud patterns, wind shifts, and animal behavior to predict weather changes. By honing these skills, we enhance our outdoor prowess and deepen our connection to the natural world, affirming the enduring relevance of these practices in modern-day exploration and survival.

CHAPTER FOUR

ECOSYSTEM ESSENTIALS & EDIBLE ENVIRONMENTS

N avigating the world of foraging encompasses more than just gathering wild foods; it's a journey through diverse environments, understanding the rhythms of weather and prioritizing safety in every step. Whether exploring lush forests, coastal shores, or urban sprawls, each environment offers unique treasures and challenges. Embarking on this foraging adventure opens doors to a deeper connection with nature and a bounty of culinary and medicinal delights while fostering respect for the environments we explore.

Understand the Environment: Climate & Terrain

Let's talk about the playground of foraging—your environment—and what you might find. It's not just about what plants are out there; it's about understanding the stage they grow on. Including the whims of weather, the drama of the terrain, and even those sneaky microclimates that could be your secret stash of goodies or a botanical wild goose chase.

Climate Factors

Have you ever noticed how some people thrive in the Miami heat while others are rejuvenating in the crisp air of the Rockies? Plants are the same; they have their preferred climates. Each region of our vast country presents a unique mix of temperature, humidity, and rainfall, significantly influencing what grows there. In the humid Southeast, you'll find lush greenery with water-loving plants like watercress thriving in abundance. Move towards the arid Southwest, and the plant life shifts to drought-tolerant species like sagebrush. Understanding these climate zones is crucial because it tells you what you will likely find and when. For instance, spring might come earlier in the warmer South than in the Northeast, affecting the availability of certain foraged items like berries or mushrooms. This knowledge prepares you for what you'll find and when you might find it, saving you from a fruitless trip (pun intended).

Terrain Analysis

Now, let's get our boots dirty and talk about the terrain. The lay of the land is more than just a backdrop for outdoor adventures; it directly affects accessibility and the abundance of resources. Steep mountains, rolling hills, dense forests, or open plains offer different foraging experiences and challenges. Hilly areas are perfect for finding morel mushrooms that prefer sloped, wooded environments. On the other hand, flat, open areas could be a haven for wild herbs and grasses. When assessing terrain, consider how easy it is to navigate. Dense underbrush or rocky grounds could make foraging a Herculean task, especially if you're hauling gear or planning a family outing. Also, consider water sources; valleys and low-lying areas near streams or rivers are often rich in plant diversity but can be tricky to access after heavy rains. In essence, your terrain shapes your foraging expedition—dictating not just what you can find but how you'll go about finding it.

Impact of Environmental Changes

If you've ever planned a beach day only to be thwarted by a sudden thunderstorm, you know that weather can be fickle. Understanding environmental changes, especially seasonal transitions and extreme weather events, is vital for foragers. These changes can affect plant growth cycles dramatically. A late frost can delay the sprouting of plants. At the same time, a sweltering summer might speed up the maturation of berries. Extreme weather events like wildfires or floods can also alter the landscape significantly, sometimes wiping out local flora or changing the soil composition, affecting future growth. Staying attuned to these changes helps in planning your foraging trips and contributes to the local ecological health by avoiding over-foraging of recovering areas.

Microclimate Considerations

Now, let's zoom in on microclimates. These are small pockets of climate conditions that differ from the surrounding areas. Think of a sunny patch on a hillside that's noticeably warmer than the shaded grove just a few feet away. These spots can be gold mines for foragers. Microclimates can support plants that wouldn't typically grow in a region, offering unique foraging opportunities. For example, a north-facing slope might retain moisture and shade longer, supporting ferns and mosses. In contrast, a south-facing slope might be drier and sunnier, ideal for sun-loving herbs. Identifying and utilizing these microclimates allows you to expand your foraging repertoire and find plants others might overlook.

Navigating the complexities of climate, terrain, environmental changes, and microclimates might seem daunting initially. Still, like any good forager, it's all about observing and adapting. With a keen eye and a bit of knowledge, you'll start to see the landscape not just as scenery but as a living, breathing guide to the treasures it holds. So, lace up those hiking boots, pack your foraging bag, and explore the vast, wildly delicious world of nature's provisions.

Foraging Through the Seasons

The timeless dance of the seasons—each turn of the calendar page ushers in new flavors hidden in our forests, meadows, and cliffs. As a seasoned forager or a budding green-thumb adventurer, aligning your foraging escapades with the rhythm of the seasons isn't just poetic—it's practical. Crafting a seasonal foraging calendar is like having a treasure map; it guides you on when to hunt for chanterelles in the dew-laden spring mornings or gather juicy blackberries as the summer sun warms the brambles.

Spring

A vibrant season for foraging as nature awakens with a bounty of flavors and textures waiting for discovery. Wild greens like tender shoots of wild garlic and nutrient-rich nettles emerge eagerly, perfect for refreshing salads or hearty soups. Early flowers such as violets and delicate elderflowers add a burst of color to dishes and infuse syrups and wines with their unique floral notes. Keep a keen eye for prized mushrooms like morels and chanterelles peeking through the forest floor, offering earthy richness to seasonal meals. Aromatic herbs like wild chives and lemon balm abound, ready to enhance culinary creations with their fresh flavors and medicinal properties.

Summer

As the wheel of seasons turns, summer brings a bounty of berries bursting with sweetness, from plump blackberries to the tang of wild raspberries, rich in antioxidants and perfect for jams or snacking. Verdant greens like lamb's quarters and dandelion add a nutritious punch to salads, stir-fries, or pesto with a wild twist. Aromatic herbs such as mint and chamomile thrive under the sun, ready to infuse teas or flavor dishes with their fragrant essence.

Autumn

When the leaves turn golden, and the air cools, woodlands and fields come alive with a new harvest. This season brings an abundance of delights, from hearty nuts like acorns and chestnuts carpeting the forest floor to vibrant berries such as elderberries and wild cranberries bursting with tart sweetness. Mushrooms like porcini emerge from their hiding places, offering earthy flavors that enrich stews and sauces—roots and tubers, like wild carrots and burdock, beckon from the earth. Herbal treasures like sage and rosemary add aromatic depth to seasonal meals. At the same time, late-season greens like dandelion leaves and chicory lend a hint of bitterness to salads.

Winter

While the landscape may appear dormant, the keen forager knows where the secrets await—watercress and chickweed brave the cold, offering fresh notes of bitterness to soups and salads. Evergreen trees, such as pine and spruce, provide nourishing needles rich in vitamin C, perfect for brewing invigorating teas that chase away the chill. Beneath the frosty ground, roots like wild parsnips and sunchokes lie dormant, their earthy sweetness ready to be unearthed and savored. Berries like rosehips and juniper berries add color and flavor to winter dishes. At the same time, nuts like hazelnuts and walnuts await discovery in leaf litter and snowy fields.

Strategies

But with the joy of seasonal abundance comes the challenge of ever-changing conditions. Each season carries its own set of weather patterns, and adapting your foraging habits accordingly can make the difference between a bountiful harvest and coming home empty-handed. After a rainfall, mushrooms tend to pop up overnight, their spores thriving in the moist soil, making post-shower excursions a must for the fungi enthusiast. On the other hand, the dry days of late summer might call for early morning ventures when the dew has settled on leaves and the day's heat hasn't yet wilted the tender plants. In the Snow-covered landscapes of winter, learning to track wildlife can be your key to uncovering winter's bounty. Deer, rabbits, and other critters can lead you to edible plants they nibble on, which remain accessible throughout the season. Spotting nibbled nutshells or digging marks can guide you to these hidden winter snacks.

With a calendar of nature's timetable in one hand and knowledge in the other, you become a master of the seasons—a forager not bound by the ebb and flow of time but one who rides its waves with expertise and anticipation. The forests, fields, and coastlines are waiting, each season with its own story to tell and flavors to share.

Seaweed and Aquatic Plants for Coastal Foragers

Ah, the salty breeze, the rhythmic lapping of the waves, and you, yes, you the intrepid coastal forager, bucket in hand, ready to dive into the oceanic garden. From the rubbery resilience of kelp to the delicate fronds of nori and the bacon-flavored delight known as dulse, these marine marvels are not just for sushi rolls—they're nutrient-packed superfoods that can jazz up your diet and even your health regimen. Before harvesting, check local regulations and obtain any necessary permits or permissions. Some areas may have restrictions on harvesting to protect marine ecosystems.

Kelp

This underwater forest giant reaches over 100 feet tall at times. Thriving in cold, nutrient-rich waters, kelp forms towering underwater columns that sway mystically with the currents. The appearance of sea kelp can vary depending on the species and environmental conditions, but generally, it has a brown or golden-brown coloration. The fronds are often broad and ribbon-like, with a sturdy central stalk called a stipe that anchors the kelp to the ocean floor. Some kelp species have pneumatocysts, gas-filled bladders that help the fronds float closer to the water surface to maximize sunlight exposure for photosynthesis.

Nori

Grows attached to rocks or other rigid substrates in intertidal zones and it thrives in areas with strong tidal currents that provide a constant flow of nutrients. They often form dense, intertidal colonies along rocky shores worldwide, particularly in temperate and cold waters. In its natural habitat, Nori appears as thin, membranous sheets that can vary in color from red to green to brown, depending on the species and environmental conditions. It's the same stuff that wraps up your sushi, but in its raw form, it has a crisp texture and a sweet, salty flavor.

Dulse

This fan favorite is a red algae that grows in cold waters along the northern coasts of the Atlantic and Pacific Oceans. It typically has a reddish-brown or purplish color and flat, somewhat leathery fronds ranging from a few inches to over a foot long. When dried, the dulse can become brittle and translucent. It's often used as a food source due to its high nutritional content and savory, salty flavor that can give your dishes a smoky, bacon-like flavor without guilt.

Harvesting

You'll want to follow the ocean's rhythms to do it sustainably and always harvest at low tide, when the seaweeds are easily accessible. Use sharp scissors to cut, not yank, the plants. This method helps preserve the root-like holdfasts, allowing the seaweed to regrow. Think of it as giving a haircut rather than pulling out the hair—ouch! Cutting just a third of the seaweed ensures the plant will continue to thrive, maintaining the underwater ecosystem and your future foraging prospects.

Why bother with these slippery sea plants? Seaweeds are nutritional powerhouses packed with vitamins, minerals, and antioxidants. They're one of the few natural sources of iodine, crucial for thyroid health, and rich in calcium, iron, and vitamin C. Plus, they contain unique compounds that can boost your heart health, reduce inflammation, and even help you manage your weight. Adding seaweeds to your diet is like hiring a team of nutritionists, all working overtime to keep you healthy.

But how do you go from beach bucket to dinner plate? Preparing and preserving seaweed is simpler than you might think. Let's take

Dulse as an example. To capture its peak flavor and nutrients, rinse the fronds in fresh water to remove grit or salt. Then, lay them out to dry. A sunny day is perfect for air-drying seaweed, but you can lay them on a baking sheet in a low-temperature oven. Once dry, dulse can be crumbled over soups, salads, or baked into healthful snacks. For a real treat, try pan-frying it until crisp—it turns into a sea vegetable bacon that will have even the most devoted carnivores asking for seconds.

There you have it: your basic guide to becoming a savvy seaweed forager. Next time you're by the coast, take a moment to explore the rocky shores and tidal pools. With scissors in hand and an eye for sustainability, you're not just collecting seaweed—you're harvesting health, flavor, and the joy of connecting with the ocean's bounty. Grab your gear, and let's make waves in your kitchen with sea-inspired delicacies!

Urban Foraging: Finding Food in the City

Suppose you're strolling through that urban jungle, far from the serene forests and quiet beaches; guess what? Mother Nature has snuck her treasures into the concrete maze, too! We're talking about urban foraging, a treasure hunt for edible plants that thrive in the city's nooks and crannies. It's like uncovering hidden gems in plain sight, and yes, even amidst the hustle and bustle, you can gather a pretty decent wild salad. But before you start plucking greens from every sidewalk crack, there are a few street-smart tips you'll want to keep in your foraging bag.

Safety

Urban environments are notorious for their not-so-plant-friendly additions, like pollutants in the soil and water runoff from roads. These can make those wild edibles less than appetizing— not to mention safe. For instance, avoiding plants from busy roadside areas or nearby known pollution sources is a good start. Parks and community gardens are usually safer bets, but remember pollutants aren't always visible. Testing the soil is your best friend when you are in doubt. Simple testing kits can reveal a lot about the soil's safety, helping you choose the best spots for foraging.

Now, onto the stars of the urban foraging scene: the plants. Oh, the variety! Dandelions, chickweed, purslane, and lamb's quarters are just a few of the urban warriors you might encounter. These plants don't just survive; they thrive in city settings, making them perfect for the budding urban forager.

Purslane

This succulent wonder often appears in garden beds and lawns. It is recognized for its fleshy, paddle-shaped leaves and small yellow flowers. Frequently considered a weed, purslane has gained popularity as a nutritious edible plant rich in omega-3 fatty acids, vitamins A, C, and B-complex, and many kinds of minerals. Its leaves have a slightly tangy and refreshing flavor and are great raw or cooked.

Lamb's Quarter

Often called wild spinach, it's a nutrient powerhouse that can be used just like its domesticated cousin. Its diamond-shaped leaves, usually coated with a frosty white powder on the undersides, stand out amidst the greenery. I love how this plant grows tall and proud, sometimes reaching several feet, adorned with clusters of tiny green flowers that add a delicate touch to its wild charm. What makes lamb's quarters truly special, despite its weed status, is being packed with vitamins A, C, and K, along with minerals like calcium and iron. Its mild, spinach-like taste makes it perfect for fresh salads, hearty soups, or simply sautéed as a nutritious side dish.

Dandelions

Though often unwelcome in well-manicured lawns, the dandelion's resilience and versatility make it a beloved plant for foragers and herbalists alike. Recognizable by their sunny yellow flowers and jagged leaves, every part of the plant is edible:

- The leaves are rich in vitamins A, C, and K and can be added to salads or cooked as greens.

- The roots can be roasted and used as a coffee substitute.

- The flowers can be turned into wine or used in culinary dishes.

Historically, dandelions have been used in herbal medicine to support liver health, improve digestion, and reduce inflammation. Found in parks, roadside patches, and even between cracks in the pavement, dandelions remind us of nature's resilience and the wealth of resources available in city life.

Urban foraging opens up a new way to view your city. Each plant you encounter tells a story of resilience and adaptability, echoing the very essence of urban life. So next time you navigate the concrete wilderness, keep your eyes peeled for those wild edibles—they might change how you see and taste your city.

Creating and Using Plant Maps

Let's talk about a secret weapon in the world of foraging—creating detailed maps of your foraging hotspots. Whether it's the sunny nook that gifts you with strawberries in the spring or the riverside path where elderberries hang ripe in the fall, mapping your foraging spots transforms your casual nature walks into targeted missions of gathering and feasting.

Start by jotting down notes or sketching maps during your foraging outings. Note what plants you find and where, and more importantly, when. This diary will soon evolve into a detailed map that reminds you of where to go and when to visit. It's like setting a dinner date with nature herself. The trick here is consistency and observation. Over time, patterns emerge, and these patterns will guide your foraging excursions, making them more predictable and fruitful.

Using GPS and Mobile Apps

Now, let's tech it up a notch! In this digital age, why rely solely on paper maps and memory when GPS technology and mobile apps can keep track of your foraging adventures? Apps like 'iNaturalist' or 'Falling Fruit' turn your smartphone into a powerful foraging tool, allowing you to mark GPS coordinates for your foraging spots. These apps often come with the added benefit of community knowledge and identification help, which means you are tracking your finds and learning from a global community of foragers.

Impact on Local Wildlife

While foraging, remember you're a guest in the home of countless wildlife species. Your actions can either help or hinder their survival. Responsible foraging practices help maintain the balance of these ecosystems. It's a practice in humility and respect, a dance with nature conducted under the vast, open skies. By foraging responsibly, you're not just harvesting ingredients but cultivating a legacy of sustainability and respect for the wild that will nourish future generations.

Conclusion

From the delicate balance of urban green spaces to the nutrient-rich coastal waters, each environment offers a unique foraging experience filled with culinary delights and medicinal treasures. Understanding these dynamics allows foragers to navigate precisely, harnessing the abundance throughout the seasons. By mindfully and responsibly exploring these diverse landscapes, you are enriching your own life and cultivating a more profound respect for the interconnectedness of ecosystems. So keep those maps handy, your apps updated, and your eyes open as we step into the food world because I'm getting hungry!

CHAPTER FIVE

WILD WONDERS: WEEDS, WILDFLOWERS, AND WELLBEING

Safe foraging practices are essential to preserve our natural landscapes and ensure the sustainability of wild edibles. Before heading out, it's crucial to accurately identify the plants you intend to gather, relying on trusted guides or expert advice. Always respect local regulations and choose clean, unpolluted areas for harvesting.

Understanding Foraging Ethics and Sustainability

Let's start with the ground rules, literally. Responsible foraging isn't just an act of sustenance; it's a pledge to preserve these landscapes, ensuring their bounty endures for generations. Unless for survival situations, it's also paramount to forage only in places where it's permitted. That lush fern sprouting in your neighbor's well-curated garden? Off-limits. Until you ask and get permission, at least. Public lands often welcome foragers, but knowing that the rules can vary widely from one park or reserve to another is crucial. Sometimes, specific permits are required, or there might be restrictions during particular seasons to protect the ecosystem. When in doubt, check it out—contact local conservation offices or park authorities to get the scoop on the green. Many communities have maps of public lands available for foraging, or you might find apps and websites dedicated to forager-friendly locations.

Essential Foraging Tools

When it comes to foraging, your equipment can be as simple or sophisticated as you like, but let's stick to the essentials to keep you agile. First up, a good knife. And no, we're not channeling Crocodile Dundee here; a simple, sturdy blade will do for slicing through stubborn stems or digging up edible roots. Next, you'll need a basket or a bag to hold your bounty. Opt for something lightweight and durable because nobody likes a bag that gives up halfway through the haul.

Remember a digging implement, a small trowel, or a sturdy stick (if you're feeling particularly savage). This little tool is a game-changer when trying to pry those stubborn, delicious tubers from the earth or digging up wild garlic like you're harvesting buried treasure.

Portable Reference Materials

Arm yourself with a couple of field guides—books or apps—that can help you identify plants accurately. Botanical keys are your ultimate cheat sheet in the plant identification exam. Think of it like playing "Guess Who?" but with plants. You'll start with broad questions—is it flowering? Are the leaves needle-like?—and with each choice, you narrow down the possibilities until voila, you've identified the plant.

Learning to use a botanical key effectively is like learning a new language. It requires practice, patience, and a bit of detective work. Once you get the hang of it though, you'll start recognizing patterns and traits that make identification quicker. The best part? There are botanical keys for different regions in the United States and around the world. Remember, the more you practice, the better you'll get. It's like leveling up in a game, where each new plant identified is a win.

Consider a waterproof notebook or any durable journal and be sure to write in pencil, so if the page gets wet the ink won't run. Documenting your finds is not just for science; it personalizes your foraging journey. Note where and when you found specific plants and how to locate them again. It is creating your map of nature's bounties.

Sensory Tests

While your eyes are your best tools, your other senses shouldn't be neglected. Let's talk about your nose and fingertips, often underrated heroes in identifying plants. Gently crushing and sniffing a leaf can reveal a hidden world of scents—from the oniony tang of wild chives to the bitter aroma of wormwood. These smells are guideposts that steer you towards edibility or warn you of nature's poisons. Touch, too, is telling. The cool, succulent feel of a plantain leaf or a nettle's rough, hairy surface delivers immediate tactile data, contributing to your growing sensory library. Remember, while your nose and fingers are fantastic tools, your mouth is not. Never taste a plant unless you're absolutely confident of its identity and safety. It's better to miss out on a wild treat than to gamble with your health.

Seasonal Variations

Understanding the rhythms of the seasons is like tuning into nature's calendar. Just as you wouldn't wear flip-flops in a snowstorm, you shouldn't expect to find spring ephemerals in the fall. Plants change throughout the year in appearance, location, and abundance. Morels, those elusive spring fungi, pop up when the earth warms, while autumn brings a bounty of nuts and seeds. Recognizing these patterns does more than boost your foraging success; it connects you with the cyclic dance of the natural world, fostering a more profound respect and appreciation for the environment and its timing.

By mastering these basic plant identification techniques, you equip yourself with the skills for successful foraging and a deeper, more intuitive connection with the natural world. Each outing becomes a chance to learn, discover, and engage with the environment meaningfully and sustainably. So, keep your eyes open, your field guide ready, and your senses tuned to the subtle whispers of the wild. Whether digging up carrots or carefully cutting away a chunk of wild honeycomb, the right tools make the task easier and infinitely more enjoyable. Remember, while technology is handy, it's no substitute for good old-fashioned knowledge and common sense.

Plant Identification Skills

Alright, you've found a promising spot and are ready to gather some wild goodies. But before you dive in, can you tell the difference between wild onion and death camas? Though they look similar, they smell very differently; one is a tasty treat, and the other is deadly. Accurate identification is the bread and butter of safe foraging. Start with leaf shapes, flower structures, and root systems. These are your clues to uncovering the identity of each plant.

Bring that reference material—these are your best friends on a foraging adventure. They'll help you match the physical characteristics of plants with pictures and descriptions. And here's a pro tip: start by learning to identify plants with no poisonous look-alikes, easing your mind a bit as you get your bearings in the foraging world. I have listed some widespread favorites across the States, but don't forget to study your specific region and microclimates.

Chickweed

Is found throughout temperate regions worldwide and often thrives in moist, shady areas like gardens, lawns, and woodland edges. It is easy to recognize by its small, star-shaped white flowers and pairs of oval-shaped, opposite leaves. Chickweed is nutritious, with a mild, slightly sweet flavor. The leaves, stems, and flowers can be eaten raw in salads or cooked as a nutritious green vegetable. Chickweed contains vitamins and minerals, including vitamins C and A, calcium, and potassium.

Clover

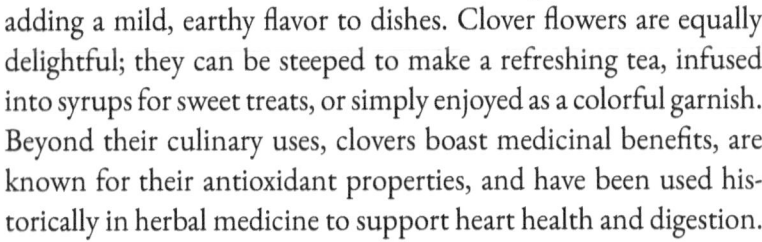

Can be found on all continents and are easily spotted by their trifoliate leaves and clusters of small, globe-shaped flowers in white, pink, or red shades. These plants are not only visually appealing but also packed with nutrients. The tender leaves can be harvested and used fresh in salads or cooked as greens, adding a mild, earthy flavor to dishes. Clover flowers are equally delightful; they can be steeped to make a refreshing tea, infused into syrups for sweet treats, or simply enjoyed as a colorful garnish. Beyond their culinary uses, clovers boast medicinal benefits, are known for their antioxidant properties, and have been used historically in herbal medicine to support heart health and digestion.

Make a Difference with Your Review

Unlock the Power of Generosity

"The best journeys answer questions that you didn't even think to ask." - Jeff Johnson

Aloha Y'all! I'm Kapena Marina and am thrilled to share the exciting journey of learning these wilderness skills and foraging techniques. We've learned so much together, and now, I have a little favor to ask.

Would you help someone you've never met, even if you never got credit for it?

My mission is to make these tips and tricks and style of learning accessible to everyone. Everything I do stems from that mission-to share Positivity and Empowerment. And the only way for me to accomplish that mission is by reaching... well... everyone.

This is where you come in. Most people do, in fact, judge a book by its cover (and its reviews). So here's my ask on behalf of a budding Survivalist you've never met:

Please help that fellow adventurer by leaving this book a review.

Your gift costs no money and less than 60 seconds, but it can change another individual's life forever. Your review could help...

...one more person learn which plants are edible in their backyard.

...one more urban dweller finds the courage to step into the wild.

...one more family enjoys the outdoors together.

...one more individual discovers the joy of self-reliance.

...one more dream of self-sufficiency comes true.

To get that 'feel good' feeling and help this person for real, all you have to do, and it takes less than 60 seconds, is...leave your opinion.

Simply scan the QR code below to leave your review:

If you feel good about helping a faceless prepping survivalist, you are my kind of person. Mahalo Nui Loa!

I'm that much more excited to help you become a more capable, resourceful, and independent individual. You'll love the tips, lessons, and strategies I'm about to share in the coming chapters.

Thank you from the bottom of my heart. Now, back to our regularly scheduled escapades into the Wilderness.

~ Your biggest fan, Kapena (which means Captain in Hawiian) and yours truly, Marina~

PS - Fun fact: If you provide something of value to another person, it makes you more valuable to them. If you know a fellow explorer—and you believe they will learn something from this information—send this book their way.

Plantain

Not the banana-like fruit, but this is a low-growing green plant that thrives in various habitats, including lawns, meadows, roadsides, and disturbed soils. The younger leaves are more suitable for salads, and older leaves are used in teas or as a poultice for insect bites and minor wounds. It is characterized by its low-growing rosette of broad, ribbed leaves that often have a slightly wavy margin. Plantain leaves vary in size but are generally lance-shaped and smooth-textured, ranging from dark green to reddish-brown. The plant produces inconspicuous flower spikes that rise above the leaves during summer. It is rich in vitamins A, C, and K, calcium, and other minerals.

Harvesting and Preparation Methods

Picking these plants isn't just about grabbing and going. There's an art to it. Timing and technique are essential to ensure you get the most out of your findings. Harvest leaves and flowers in the morning after the dew has dried but before the sun is high—when their essential oils are most potent. Roots are best harvested in the fall when the plant's energy is concentrated below ground. Always cut with a clean, sharp knife or scissors to avoid bruising the plant tissues, which can lead to loss of beneficial oils and increased risk of decay.

Toxic Plants to Avoid

Nature is only sometimes marked with warning signs, so it's up to you to know the hazards. Be aware of poisonous plants and harmful insects native to your area. Protective clothing, like long sleeves and sturdy pants, can shield you from scratches, bug bites, and the rash-inducing wrath of plants like poison oak.

Navigating nature's no-no list starts with getting to know the usual suspects. Each region has its lineup of toxic plants, but some universal troublemakers love to pop up everywhere.

Water Hemlock

Considered one of the most toxic plants in North America; it commonly grows in wet areas like marshes, riverbanks, and ditches. It can be identified by its umbrella-like clusters of small white flowers, finely divided leaves, and distinctive, hollow, chambered stems often streaked with purple. All parts of the plant, especially the roots, contain cicutoxin. This potent neurotoxin can cause severe and often fatal seizures if ingested. Due to its extreme toxicity, it's crucial to recognize and avoid water hemlock when foraging or spending time in natural, wet environments.

Poison Ivy

Common just about everywhere in North, Central, and South America, poison ivy is easily recognizable by its clusters of three glossy green leaflets that can turn red in the fall. It often grows as a low shrub or climbing vine.

The plant produces an oily resin called urushiol, which can cause a severe, itchy, and blistering rash upon contact with the skin. Poison ivy thrives in shaded and sunny areas in forests, fields, and roadsides.

Poison Oak

Primarily found in the Western United States and parts on North Mexico, it can be recognized by its trifoliate leaf pattern similar to that of Poison Ivy, with leaves ranging in color from green in the spring and summer to red, orange, or yellow in the fall. This plant grows as a shrub and a climbing vine, often found in wooded areas, along trails, and sunny spots. All plant parts, including the stems and roots, contain urushiol and can cause a reaction year-round, even when the plant appears dormant.

Foxglove

A strikingly beautiful but highly toxic plant native to Europe and Scandinavia, it can now be found in North America, New Zealand, and Australia. Commonly seen in gardens, woodlands, and along roadsides, it is noticeable for its tall spikes adorned with tubular, bell-shaped flowers in shades of purple, pink, white, and yellow. The plant's leaves, flowers, and seeds contain cardiac glycosides, such as digitalis and digitoxin, which can cause severe and potentially fatal heart problems if ingested.

Symptoms of Poisoning

So, you accidentally brushed up against something you shouldn't have, or perhaps curiosity got the better of you, leading to an impromptu taste test. What now? Recognizing the symptoms of plant poisoning can be crucial. Symptoms can range from mildly irritating, such as itching or rashes from poison ivy, to severe, like nausea, seizures, vomiting, diarrhea, or even death from ingesting something as lethal as water hemlock.

The first step in any potential poisoning is to stay calm. If possible, identify the culprit and clean the affected area with soap and water to remove any plant oils or residues. If symptoms escalate or if ingested, seek medical help immediately. Remember, time is of the essence, and accurately describing the plant or, better yet, showing a picture or sample to medical professionals can make all the difference.

Myths and Misconceptions

Now, onto some myth-busting! How often have you heard someone say, "It's okay to eat this; I saw a bird do it!"? Well, friend, you must suddenly sprout feathers and a beak to make this a reliable test. Animals and humans react differently to various substances, so what's safe for a squirrel or a bird might not be safe for you. Another popular myth is that boiling or cooking a plant can remove toxins. Doing so is true for some but definitely not for all. Plants like elderberry can be toxic raw but are perfectly safe when cooked. However, others keep their lethal traits no matter how much you boil them.

Safety Protocols

When in doubt, leave it out. Only consume a plant if you are 100% sure of its identity and edibility. Equip yourself with a good field guide or a foraging app to help make informed decisions. Always have a specialized first aid kit on hand, one that includes treatments for allergic reactions and basic first aid supplies. It's a small addition that could be a lifesaver, turning a potential disaster into an exciting story.

Conclusion

Foraging combines preparation, observation, and respect for nature's offerings. Equipped with essential tools and a keen eye for
plant identification, you can confidently navigate the wilderness
and gather treasures that range from culinary delights to medicinal remedies. However, vigilance is crucial; always be mindful of
potentially harmful species and stay informed through reliable resources. With knowledge as your shield and caution as your guide,
you're all set to forage safely, steering clear of nature's no-nos while
enjoying the plethora of plants on the menu.

Chapter Six

FIRST AID FUNDAMENTALS FOR FEARLESS FIELD CARE

A bit of knowledge can be a lifeline in the great outdoors. This Chapter is all about being aware and understanding some essential first-aid techniques, practical strategies for preventing infection, and the incredible power of natural remedies using herbs. Whether you're an avid hiker, a weekend camper, or someone who simply loves spending time in nature, understanding how to handle injuries and illnesses without modern conveniences is invaluable. We'll cover everything from treating common cuts and scrapes, managing blisters, and soothing insect bites to recognizing and addressing more severe concerns like dehydration and heat exhaustion.

Tips for Outdoor Survival

Venturing into the wild offers a sense of freedom and connection to nature that's hard to match. But with that freedom comes the responsibility to be prepared for the unexpected. Scrapes, burns, bites, and sprains are part of the package deal of adventuring in the wild. Knowing basic first aid can make all the difference in an emergency, whether hiking, camping, or embarking on a more extended wilderness adventure. Here's a guide to essential first aid skills and supplies to help you handle common injuries and illnesses in the wild.

Building Your Wilderness Kit

Before heading out, ensure your first aid kit is well-stocked. Here are the must-have items:

Bandages and Dressings:

- **Adhesive Bandages:** Pack a variety of sizes to cover minor cuts and scrapes. These are also great for blisters.

- **Sterile Gauze Pads:** These are useful for covering larger wounds and controlling bleeding. I have several 4x4-inch pads.

- **Adhesive Tape:** To secure gauze pads and bandages in place. A roll of paper tape should suffice.

- **Elastic Bandage (ACE Wrap):** This is essential for wrapping sprains and securing splints. Choose a medium-width bandage.

Antiseptics:

- **Antiseptic Wipes or Solution:** Hydrogen peroxide or iodine wipes are great for cleaning wounds.

- **Antibiotic Ointment:** A small tube of Aquaphor, Neosporin, or similar ointment helps prevent infection in minor cuts.

Medications:

- **Pain Relievers:** Bring both ibuprofen (anti-inflammatory) and acetaminophen (Tylenol) for pain and fever.

- **Antihistamines:** Benadryl is helpful for allergic reactions to insect bites or plant contact.

- **Anti-Diarrheal Medication:** Imodium can be a lifesaver if you encounter digestive issues.

- **Personal Prescription Medications:** Ensure you have enough of any personal medications you need, plus a little extra.

Tools and Equipment:

- **Tweezers:** For removing splinters, ticks, or other small foreign objects.

- **Scissors:** A small pair for cutting tape, gauze, or clothing.

- **Safety Pins:** For securing bandages or slings.

- **Thermometer:** A compact digital thermometer can help monitor for fever.

Other Essentials:

- **Moleskin or Blister Pads:** To prevent and treat blisters on feet.

- **Emergency Blanket:** Mylar blankets are lightweight and can prevent hypothermia.

- **Instant Cold Packs:** To reduce swelling from injuries.

- **Splinting Materials:** A SAM splint is compact and versatile, but even a sturdy stick can work in a pinch.

Common Wilderness Injuries

Let's start with the basics. Nature, while beautiful, doesn't always love us back. Scrapes, burns, bites, and sprains are part of the package deal of adventuring in the wild. Knowing how to handle these mishaps effectively can mean distinguishing between a minor setback and a ruined outing.

- Start by cleaning the wound thoroughly.

- Use clean water from your bottle that you so expertly filtered from Chapter 2 and rinse away any dirt and debris.

- Apply an antiseptic solution like hydrogen peroxide or iodine for disinfection.

- Secure a sterile gauze pad over the wound with adhesive tape.

- Change the dressing daily and keep the wound clean to promote healing and prevent infection.

Blisters

Blisters are common, especially on long hikes. Prevention is key:

- Wear moisture-wicking socks and shoes that fit correctly. If you know you'll be walking a lot, consider applying moleskin to high-friction areas before you start.

- If a blister forms, gently clean the area and apply an antibiotic ointment to prevent infection.

- Cover with a blister pad or moleskin to protect it. If it is particularly large or painful, you may need to sterilize a needle with a flame and pierce the blister to drain the fluid.

Sprains and Strains

Sprains and strains can occur from slips, trips, or overexertion. The first step in treatment is rest. Stop using the injured limb and give it time to heal. Apply an instant cold pack or wrap ice in a cloth and place it on the injured area for 20 minutes every hour. This helps reduce swelling and pain. To further reduce swelling, wrap the area with an elastic bandage, but ensure it's not too tight to avoid restricting blood flow. Elevate the injured limb above heart level whenever possible to minimize swelling. Think RICE- Rest, Ice, Compression, Elevation.

Insect Bites and Stings

Insect bites and stings are common in the wild. If you get stung, use tweezers to remove any stingers left in the skin gently. Clean the area with soap and water to prevent infection. Applying a cold pack to the bite or sting for 10-15 minutes can help reduce swelling and pain. It's essential to monitor for signs of a severe allergic reaction, such as difficulty breathing or swelling of the face or throat. If these symptoms occur, use an epinephrine injector if available and seek emergency help immediately. Taking an antihistamine like Benadryl or homeopathic apis mellifica for milder reactions can help alleviate symptoms.

Burns

Burns are classified into three categories based on their severity. First-degree burns affect the outer layer of the skin, causing redness and mild pain. Second-degree burns penetrate deeper, resulting in blisters, severe pain, and potential swelling. Third-degree burns are the most severe, damaging all skin layers and possibly underlying tissues, often appearing charred or white. Immediate action is crucial for treating burns in the wilderness. Quickly remove the person from the heat source to prevent further injury. As soon as possible, apply lavender oil, if available, and cool the burn with cool (not cold) running water for 10-15 minutes to reduce pain and avoid more profound tissue damage. If water isn't available, a cool, wet compress can suffice. Protect the burn by loosely covering it with a sterile, non-stick bandage or clean cloth to prevent infection. Look around for aloe vera, which can provide soothing relief and aid healing. Over-the-counter pain relievers such as ibuprofen can help manage discomfort. Seek medical attention for second-degree burns more significant than 3 inches in diameter or any third-degree burn to ensure proper care and treatment.

Heat Exhaustion and Heat Stroke

Heat-related illnesses can be severe and require prompt attention. For heat exhaustion, move to a shaded area, remove excess clothing, and cool down with wet cloths or a cool bath if possible. It's crucial to hydrate by drinking plenty of water or an electrolyte solution. Avoid caffeine and alcohol as they can worsen dehydration. Monitor for symptoms of heat stroke, such as confusion, high body temperature, and lack of sweating. If heat stroke is suspected, seek immediate medical attention and continue efforts to cool the person down.

Hypothermia

Hypothermia occurs when the body loses heat faster than it can produce it. To treat hypothermia, move the affected person to a warm, dry place. Remove any wet clothing and replace it with dry, insulating layers. Use blankets, sleeping bags, and body heat to warm the person. An emergency blanket can help retain body heat effectively. If the person is conscious and able to drink, provide warm, non-alcoholic, and non-caffeinated drinks to help increase their core temperature.

Essential Skills

CPR

Knowing how to perform CPR can be lifesaving. Take a certified course to learn the proper technique. Remember, you're not trying to be perfect—you're trying to help save a life, and every bit counts.

Here's how to get started:

1. **Check for responsiveness**: Tap the person's shoulder and shout to see if they respond. If they don't respond and are not breathing normally, call for help or tell someone nearby to dial 911.

2. **Start chest compressions**: Place the heel of one hand in the center of the person's chest, right between the nipples. Put your other hand on top and interlace your fingers. Push hard and fast, aiming for a rate of 100-120 compressions per minute. You want to press down at least 2 inches deep. Think of it like a steady beat—songs like "Stayin' Alive" have the perfect CPR rhythm.

3. **Rescue breaths** (if trained): After 30 compressions, give two rescue breaths. Tilt the head back slightly, lift the chin, pinch the nose, and breathe into their mouth until you see their chest rise. Focus on continuous compressions if you're uncomfortable with breaths or un-trained.

4. **Keep going**: Don't stop until emergency help arrives or the person starts breathing independently. Your effort could make all the difference even if you're tired.

Wound Care

Keeping wounds clean, preventing infection, and promoting healing are your top health priorities in the wild. Practice cleaning
wounds thoroughly and learn how to apply different types of
bandages. Knowing when to use adhesive bandages, gauze pads,
and elastic bandages can make a significant difference in managing
wounds effectively.

Splinting

Learning how to immobilize a fractured or sprained limb using a
splint is a valuable skill. To create a makeshift splint, use items like
a SAM splint, sticks, or even a rolled-up blanket. Secure it with an
elastic bandage or cloth strips to stabilize the injury and prevent
further damage.

Choking Response

Understanding the Heimlich maneuver for clearing airway ob-
structions is crucial. Stand behind the person, wrap your arms
around their waist, and give quick, upward thrusts just above the
navel until the object is expelled. This technique can save a life in
choking emergencies.

Staying Safe

Know Your Limits: Understand your physical capabilities and
don't push beyond them. Plan your activities according to your
fitness level and experience.

Stay Informed: Be aware of the weather and terrain you'll be
encountering. Check forecasts and trail conditions before you set
out.

Communicate: Let someone know your plans and expected return time. Use a GPS device or a personal locator beacon (PLB) if you're going into remote areas.

Trust Your Instincts: If something feels wrong, it probably is. Don't ignore signs of injury or illness. It is better to be cautious than to risk worsening the situation.

Being prepared with first aid knowledge and a well-equipped kit can turn a potentially dangerous situation into a manageable one. Remember, the wild is unpredictable, but with the proper preparation, you can handle whatever comes your way. Stay safe, stay informed, and enjoy your adventures in the great outdoors! Consider taking an introductory first aid course or at least familiarizing yourself with online resources. Mastering these skills isn't just about being safe. It's about stepping confidently into any situation, knowing you're prepared to handle whatever happens.

Nature's Medicine Cabinet

For those of you who like a holistic side to your practice, nature's not just the cause of our woes but also a provider of cures. Nature itself provides a bounty of remedies that can complement your first aid kit. Here's a guide to using natural remedies for first aid in the wild and in your home, blending modern knowledge with traditional wisdom.

Aloe Vera: All Inclusive Natural Wellness and Beauty

Widely renowned for its numerous natural benefits, both for internal and external use. Here are the key benefits:

- **Skin Healing**: Has anti-inflammatory and antimicrobial properties that accelerate the healing of cuts, burns, and sunburns.

- **Moisturizing**: Hydrates and nourishes the skin, making it an excellent natural moisturizer.

- **Digestive Health**: Aloe Vera juice aids digestion, relieving constipation and soothing the digestive tract.

- **Anti-Inflammatory**: Reduces inflammation internally and externally, relieving conditions like arthritis and skin irritations.

- **Immune Support**: Rich in antioxidants, it boosts the immune system and protects against oxidative stress.

To harvest and preserve Aloe Vera, begin by selecting mature, thick leaves from the outer sections of the plant. Cut the leaves close to the base using a clean, sharp knife. Allow the cut leaves to sit upright for a few minutes to let the yellow latex drain out, as it can be irritating. Once drained, wash the leaves thoroughly. Cut away the thick skin to preserve and scoop out the clear gel. Store the gel in an airtight container in the refrigerator for up to a week or freeze it in ice cube trays for longer storage.

Willow Bark: Nature's Aspirin

Willow bark has been used for centuries as a natural pain reliever due to salicin, chemically similar to aspirin (acetylsalicylic acid).

- **Pain Relief:** The salicin in the bark is metabolized in the body to produce salicylic acid, which reduces inflammation and alleviates discomfort.

- **Anti-Inflammatory:** This makes it helpful in treating joint pain, arthritis, and other inflammatory conditions. It can also help manage minor injuries like sprains and strains.

- **Fever Reduction:** Similar to aspirin, it can be used to reduce fever and help with flu symptoms.

How to Identify, Harvest, and Utilize

Willow trees, particularly the white willow, are most commonly used for medicinal purposes. They grow near water sources like rivers and lakes, and have long, slender leaves and rough, grayish bark. Collect from young, thin branches or twigs, not damaging the tree by removing too much bark from one area. Peel off the outer layer to access the inner bark, which contains the beneficial compounds.

For a simple remedy, make willow bark tea by boiling a small handful of inner bark in water for 10-15 minutes, then steeping for another 10 minutes. Strain and drink the tea 2-3 times daily for pain relief. If boiling water isn't an option, you can chew the fresh inner bark directly, though it may be bitter. This method provides immediate relief from pain and inflammation. Alternatively, grind the inner bark into a paste with water and apply it topically as a compress to inflamed or painful areas to help reduce swelling and discomfort.

Whether you're dealing with a headache, sore muscles, or a mild fever, this powerful plant offers pain relief and anti-inflammatory benefits, making it an essential part of any natural survival toolkit. Just be mindful of proper identification and dosage, and you'll have a reliable, effective way to treat common ailments using nature's aspirin.

Honey: Nature's Sweetener

 Referred to as liquid gold, it is more than just a sweet treat; it's a powerhouse of health benefits. From ancient times to modern-day uses, honey has earned its place in natural remedies and wellness routines.

- **Wound Healing**: Has antibacterial properties that promote faster healing of cuts, burns, and abrasions.

- **Skin Care**: Moisturizes and soothes the skin, effectively treating acne and maintaining a healthy complexion.

- **Digestive Health**: Aids digestion, alleviating indigestion and soothing the digestive tract.

- **Immune Boosting**: Rich in antioxidants, honey strengthens the immune system and combats oxidative stress.

- **Cough Relief**: It is a natural cough suppressant, relieving sore throats and cold symptoms.

Incorporating honey into your daily routine, whether as a sweetener, a topical treatment, or a natural remedy, can offer a wide range of health benefits. Remember to use your hands when collecting in the wild and carefully break off small pieces of the honeycomb. Be gentle to minimize damage to the hive and avoid angering the bees.

Honey can also be used in DIY face masks and skincare routines for its hydrating and antioxidant benefits. Also, it is very important to note that it should not be given to infants under one year due to the risk of botulism.

Herbal Remedies

Nature's way of offering us a gentle, yet powerful, approach to our health and healing. These natural treatments are derived from plants and plant extracts, such as herbs, flowers, roots, and leaves, and have been used for centuries to address various health conditions. They offer an alternative to synthetic medications, tapping into the rich medicinal properties of the natural world.

Herbal remedies come in many forms—teas, tinctures, salves, and capsules—and they're incredibly versatile. Whether it's boosting the immune system, easing digestive issues, or treating skin conditions, these natural solutions support overall wellness in a gentle, sustainable manner. Accurate plant identification and consultation with knowledgeable sources are essential steps to ensure safety and efficacy in using natural remedies. By doing so, you can confidently and responsibly embrace the benefits of nature's pharmacy.

Chamomile:

- **Calming Effects**: Renowned for its soothing properties, effectively reduces anxiety and promotes relaxation.

- **Sleep Aid**: Acts as a mild sedative, helps to improve sleep quality and treat insomnia.

- **Digestive Health**: Alleviates digestive issues like indigestion, gas, and stomach cramps.

- **Anti-Inflammatory**: Reduces inflammation and can be used to treat conditions like arthritis and skin irritations.

- **Skin Health**: Soothes the skin and treats eczema, rashes, and minor wounds.

Chamomile is generally safe for consumption and can be enjoyed as a tea or applied topically. However, those with allergies to plants in the daisy family should use it cautiously.

Ginger:

- **Digestive Aid**: Soothes digestive issues like nausea, indigestion, and stomach cramps.

- **Seasickness:** Helps with seasickness primarily due to its natural anti-emetic (anti-nausea) properties. So, before the next voyage grab a piece of raw ginger, supplements, or a bag of organic chewy candies, because it really does help.

- **Anti-Inflammatory**: Reduces inflammation and can be used to alleviate conditions such as arthritis and sore throats.

- **Antimicrobial**: Possesses antimicrobial properties, making it helpful in treating infections and preventing bacterial growth.

- **Pain Relief**: It is a natural analgesic relieving headaches, toothaches, and other minor pains.

- **Respiratory Health**: Help relieve respiratory issues like congestion and bronchitis due to its expectorant properties.

Ginger can be used in teas, tinctures, or as a poultice. However, it should be used in moderation and with caution, as exorbitantly high doses can be toxic.

Comfrey:

- **Anti-Inflammatory**: Reduces inflammation and swelling, relieves conditions like arthritis and muscle strains.

- **Wound Healing**: Known to promote rapid cell regeneration, effectively treats cuts, bruises, and minor injuries.

- **Bone Health**: Contains allantoin, which supports the repair of bone fractures and sprains.

- **Skin Health**: Soothes and hydrates the skin, aiding in the treatment of conditions like eczema and psoriasis.

- **Pain Relief**: Is a natural analgesic that alleviates pain when applied topically.

Despite its benefits, comfrey should be used cautiously and only externally, as it contains compounds that can be toxic to the liver when ingested.

Peppermint:

- **Digestive Aid**: Soothes digestive issues such as indigestion, bloating, and gas and can help alleviate symptoms of IBS (irritable bowel syndrome).

- **Pain Relief**: Its analgesic properties help

reduce headaches, muscle pain, and menstrual cramps when applied topically or inhaled.

- **Respiratory Health**: The menthol content helps clear respiratory passages, effectively relieving colds, congestion, and sinusitis.

- **Mental Clarity**: Inhaling peppermint oil can enhance concentration, improve mental clarity, and reduce fatigue.

- **Antimicrobial**: Has antimicrobial properties that help combat bacteria and fungi, supporting oral health and freshening breath.

Peppermint is a versatile herb that can be incorporated into daily routines through various forms such as tea, essential oils, and fresh leaves. However, it should be used with caution by individuals with gastroesophageal reflux disease (GERD), as it may exacerbate symptoms.

Thyme:

- **Antimicrobial Properties**: It is effective against bacteria, fungi, and viruses, making it helpful in treating infections and boosting immunity.

- **Respiratory Health**: Alleviates respiratory conditions like coughs, bronchitis, and asthma due to its antispasmodic and expectorant qualities.

- **Digestive Aid**: Supports digestion by relieving indigestion, bloating, and gas and promoting overall health.

- **Anti-Inflammatory**: Reduces inflammation, relieving conditions such as arthritis and muscle pain.

- **Antioxidant-Rich**: Packed with antioxidants, which protect the body from oxidative stress and promote overall wellness.

Thyme can be used fresh or dried in cooking or brewed as a tea. It is generally safe for consumption but should be used in moderation, especially by individuals with allergies to the mint family.

Turmeric:

- **Anti-Inflammatory**: Contains curcumin, a potent anti-inflammatory compound that reduces inflammation and pain in conditions like arthritis.

- **Antioxidant**: Rich in antioxidants that protect the body from free radicals and oxidative stress, boosting overall health.

- **Digestive Health**: Aids in digestion, alleviates bloating, and supports liver function.

- **Brain Health:** Supports cognitive function and mental clarity, helps reduce the risk of neurodegenerative diseases, such as Alzheimer's, and can improve mood by boosting serotonin and BDNF levels.

- **Immune Support**: Enhances the immune system, helping to ward off infections and illnesses.

- **Heart Health**: Improves cardiovascular health by reducing cholesterol levels and improving blood vessel function.

Turmeric can be used in cooking, taken as a supplement, or applied topically for skin benefits. For best results, combine it with black pepper to enhance curcumin absorption.

Essential Oils

Moving on to something a bit more refined. Essential oils are concentrated plant essences and can be powerful allies in your natural medicine cabinet. Safety first, though! Essential oils are potent, and a little goes a long way. Always dilute them in a carrier oil like coconut or almond oil before applying directly to the skin to avoid irritation. The only exception is for a burn. Apply full-strength lavender oil directly to the affected area as soon as possible!

Lavender is well-known for its calming and relaxing properties, effectively reducing stress, anxiety, and depression and promoting restful sleep. Its antimicrobial properties make it helpful in treating cuts, burns, and skin irritations, promoting faster healing. Lavender oil also has potent anti-inflammatory and analgesic qualities, helping to soothe muscle aches, joint pain, and headaches. It is great for homemade skin care, hair care, and cleaning products. If you have room for only one essential oil, make it this one!

Tea Tree Oil is highly valued for its potent antimicrobial properties, making it effective against bacteria, viruses, and fungi. It promotes skin health by treating acne, reducing inflammation, and healing minor cuts and wounds. Tea tree oil can disinfect surfaces and purify the air as a natural antiseptic. It also supports oral health by helping to combat bad breath and prevent infections by adding a few drops to a glass of warm water and swishing like a mouthwash. Tea tree oil's anti-inflammatory properties also relieve muscle aches and joint pain. At the same time, its refreshing scent helps invigorate the mind, reducing stress and improving mood, focus, and mental clarity.

Clove has analgesic properties that provide effective pain relief, particularly for toothaches and sore muscles. The oil's strong antimicrobial qualities make it excellent for fighting off bacterial, viral, and fungal infections. Its anti-inflammatory properties help reduce swelling and discomfort in conditions like arthritis.

Eucalyptus is highly effective in promoting respiratory health by clearing nasal congestion, soothing coughs, and alleviating symptoms of bronchitis and asthma. Its anti-inflammatory and analgesic properties make it helpful in relieving muscle and joint pain. As an antimicrobial agent, eucalyptus oil can help fight off bacterial, viral, and fungal infections. It also supports the immune system, enhancing the body's natural defense mechanisms. Additionally, eucalyptus oil has a refreshing and invigorating scent that can boost mental clarity and reduce stress.

Tapping into the Rewards

There are plenty of options for turning these plants into remedies. Teas are the easiest, requiring steeping the leaves or flowers in hot water for about 10 minutes. While creating tinctures, salves, and poultices might sound like you need a chemistry set, it's surprisingly straightforward and as rewarding as it is practical.

Creating a Salve

Starts with infusing herbs into a carrier oil, such as olive or coconut oil. Gently heat the cleaned herbs and oil together, letting them meld their properties over low heat for several hours. Once infused, strain the herbs and mix the oil with melted beeswax to create a smooth, creamy consistency. Pour the mixture into small jars letting it cool and solidify into a soothing salve that's perfect for cuts, scrapes, or dry skin.

Poultices

These are immediate remedies, ideal for soothing inflammation or drawing out toxins. Start by crushing fresh or dried herbs with a mortar and pestle, creating a thick, herbal paste. Adding a bit of warm water or oil helps to bind it together. Apply this poultice directly to the affected area, cover it with a clean cloth or bandage, letting the herbs work their magic for about 20-30 minutes. It's a simple yet effective way to provide relief from bruises, insect bites, or even minor burns.

Making a Tincture

Capturing the essence of nature's remedies in a bottle. After gathering the bounty, rinse them gently to remove any dirt. Ensure to chop as finely as possible to expose more surface area. Then, they go into a clean glass jar, filling it about halfway. Next comes the alcohol—typically vodka or brandy of the strongest proof—pouring enough to cover the herbs completely. Seal the jar tightly and give it a good shake. This concoction will sit in a cool, dark place for a few weeks, occasionally shake it to encourage the alcohol to draw out the plant's beneficial compounds. When the time's right, strain the liquid through cheesecloth. The result? A potent herbal tincture, ready to soothe a sore throat or calm a restless night, crafted with your own hands and nature's generosity. For those who prefer not to use alcohol- vinegar or glycerin are excellent alternatives. However, they might not extract as wide a range of compounds.

Armed with your tinctures, teas, and salves, let's tackle some common ailments. Peppermint or licorice tea can be an excellent soother for an upset stomach. A salve made from calendula or

plantain leaf, known for its soothing, anti-inflammatory properties, can be a relief for skin irritations. And if you're dealing with
a pesky cough, a shot of tincture made from thyme, which acts as
an expectorant, can help clear your airways.

Safety and Dosage Considerations

Before you go wild and start concocting your natural remedies,
a word to the wise: moderation is essential, and informed usage
is non-negotiable. With dosage —more is not always better. Start
small, especially if it's a plant you haven't used before, to see how
your body reacts. And always, always double-check for potential
interactions with any other medications you might be taking.

For instance, while St. John's Wort is renowned for helping with
mild depression, it can interfere with the efficacy of prescription
medications. If you're pregnant, nursing, or preparing remedies for
children, consult with a healthcare provider before adding any new
herbal remedies to your regimen. Nature is powerful; use it wisely
to enhance your health and well-being.

With some knowledge and respect, you can tap into the ancient
wisdom of plants. So, next time you're out in your garden or
walking through a park, keep your eyes peeled for these natural
wonders. Your very own health revolution might just be growing
underfoot!

Acupressure Techniques

Sometimes, the simplest remedies are literally at our fingertips. Acupressure, an ancient healing technique from traditional
Chinese medicine, involves applying pressure to specific points on the body, which
can stimulate the body's natural self-cu-
rative abilities. You can perform it with
just your hands; no equipment necessary.
Suffering from a tension headache? Press

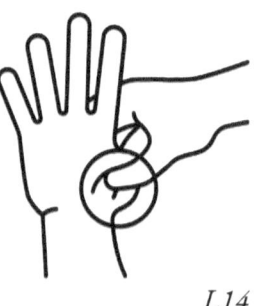

LI4

firmly with your thumb or finger between your opposite hand's
thumb and index finger (this spot is called LI4) for about a minute.
Nausea from that bumpy off-road driving? Find point PC6, about
three fingers width down from the wrist on the inner forearm and
press gently. It's like having a reset button for your body, and the
best part is it's always with you.

Conclusion

First aid isn't just about applying bandages or knowing CPR
(though those are important, too!). It's about being prepared to
handle unexpected situations, from minor cuts and bruises to
more severe injuries. So, if you really want to be prepared, be sure
to explore and learn how to use these alternative healing aids now.
Remember that your health and wellness tools might not always
come in a pill bottle or a box, but all around you, in the leaves, oils,
and even in the pressure of your touch.

CHAPTER SEVEN

BACKWOODS BISTRO AND SUSTAINABLE SUPPERS

Welcome to the rustic adventure of off-grid cuisine, where solar cookers bake bread with golden crusts and crackling fires infuse smoked meats with deep, savory notes. So, whether crafting a sun-kissed dessert or savoring the smoky richness of a slow-cooked feast, may each bite remind you of the joy and simplicity of off-grid cooking.

Preparing Meals with an Open Fire

Let's talk about the timeless art of cooking over an open fire, where each flame dances to the tune of ancient culinary secrets. It's not just about roasting marshmallows or singing campfire songs (though those are undoubtedly fun perks). It's about mastering the primal essence of fire to create mouthwatering meals that would make even a caveman chef proud. Whether in your backyard or out in the wild, knowing how to build and manage a cooking fire is a skill that'll spice up your outdoor adventures.

Fundamentals of Fire Building

First things first, let's spark up some knowledge on building a proper cooking fire. You might think any old pile of burning wood will do, but how the subtleties matter! You might consider several fire lays, each with its charm. The teepee fire, with its conical structure, is a go-to for its ease of lighting and airiness, perfect for a quick grill. The log cabin lay, with its structured stack of logs, offers a stable, enduring burn, ideal for slow cooking and warmth. And let's not forget the pyramid lay, where logs are stacked in a square, ascending pattern – think of it as the slow-cooker of fire lays, providing a steady, lasting heat.

Managing the heat of your open fire is an art form in itself. Unlike your predictable kitchen stove, fire is dynamic and influenced by wind, fuel type, and setup. Spreading coals allows for a broader, more even cooking surface, reducing hot spots that could burn your food. Adjusting the height of your grill or pot can also help manage the cooking temperature—higher for slower cooking and lower for searing heat. And remember, different woods burn at different temperatures; cherry wood imparts a medium heat perfect for baking, while mesquite's intense burn is ideal for grilling steaks.

Safety is not just a suggestion when using fire—it's a must. Always clear the area of flammable materials and ensure your fire site is surrounded by non-combustible dirt or stones. Choosing the right fuel is crucial, too; seasoned hardwoods like oak or hickory offer a long, consistent burn, while softer woods like pine will burn faster but with more smoke—not ideal when you're trying not to smoke out the food or yourself.

Techniques and Equipment

One of the joys of cooking outdoors is experimenting with primitive techniques. Here are a few versatile methods to try:

- **Direct-fire cooking**: Place food directly on a grill made from green branches or suspend it above the flames using a tripod. This method is great for meats, fish, or skewered vegetables.

- **Stone Cooking**: Heat flat rocks in your fire and use them as a cooking surface. You can fry eggs, cook flatbreads, or roast meats on a hot stone.

- **Cooking in Leaves**: Wrap food in large, non-toxic leaves before placing it on hot coals or in a steaming pit. This method protects the food from ash and adds a subtle flavor.

- **Pit Cooking**: Dig a hole, line it with hot stones, and layer your food with leaves for insulation. Cover it with soil and let it slow-cook for hours—ideal for large cuts of meat or root vegetables.

- **Stick Roasting**: Use green sticks to skewer food like fish, sausages, or dough twisted into spirals. Hold them over the fire for a simple, hands-on approach.

Leaves are nature's cookware, ideal for lining, wrapping, or even serving food.

- **Burdock Leaves**: Found in temperate zones, burdock leaves are large and durable. They're excellent for lining containers or wrapping food for steaming. Clean them thoroughly and use fresh leaves to avoid bitter taste.

- **Grape Leaves**: These edible leaves are perfect for wrapping food, similar to how they're used to make dolmas. They're pliable and add a mild, tangy flavor when cooked.

- **Corn Husks**: If you're near a cornfield or wild maize,

husks make a great alternative to leaves. They can be used to line or wrap food for grilling or boiling.

- **Banana Leaves**: In tropical regions, banana leaves are a go-to for cooking. They're large, sturdy, and naturally waterproof. Use them to wrap food for steaming or grilling or to line a pit for cooking Hot Stone Soup. They also impart a subtle, earthy flavor to the food.

- **Oak and Maple Leaves**: These are durable and widely available in temperate climates. While not edible, they can line cooking holes or serve as a makeshift platter.

Hot Stone Soup

This is a bushcraft classic that showcases ingenuity and simplicity. This method uses heated stones to boil water in a container made from natural materials like wood, bark, or even the earth itself. It's a versatile recipe that adapts to your environment, relying on foraged or packed ingredients and basic cooking techniques.

To begin, gather your ingredients. You'll need fresh water, vegetables like wild greens, cattail roots, or packed options such as carrots and potatoes, and a source of protein—freshly caught fish, small game, or even jerky. Seasonings like wild thyme, sage, or rosemary can add flavor, and optional add-ins like mushrooms or nuts enhance the nutrition and taste.

Prepare your container, which can be a hollowed-out wooden bowl, bark container, or even a hole in the ground lined with waterproof leaves.

The next step is heating your stones. Choose medium-sized, clean stones free of cracks or moisture to avoid explosions when they heat up. Place the stones in your fire and let them heat for at least 30 minutes until red-hot. While the stones heat, place your prepared ingredients into the container, covering them with fresh water. Once the stones are ready, carefully transfer them to the container using sticks or tongs. The hot stones will cause the water to boil, creating the perfect environment to cook your soup.

Let the soup simmer, and if the water temperature drops, add additional hot stones to maintain the heat. In about 15-20 minutes, your ingredients should be tender and fully cooked. When the soup is ready, remove the stones with a stick or tongs and allow the soup to cool slightly before serving. Use a cup or a large leaf to ladle out servings and enjoy your hot, hearty meal.

To ensure success, always choose non-porous stones to avoid cracking, purify your water if needed, and forage carefully to ensure all plants and herbs are edible. The beauty of Hot Stone Soup lies in its adaptability—each pot can be as unique as the environment you're in, offering endless opportunities to experiment with flavors.

Bannock Bread

Simple and a staple in many cultures, especially among Indigenous peoples of North America and Scotland. Made with just a few ingredients, it's a favorite for bushcraft enthusiasts and survivalists alike.

To prepare Bannock, mix one cup of flour (foraged or packed), one teaspoon of baking powder (optional), 1/4 teaspoon of salt (if available), one tablespoon of fat (butter, oil, or animal fat), and 1/3 cup of water. Stir until the dough comes together, knead briefly, and shape it into a flat disk about 1/2 inch thick. Optional add-ins like wild berries, chopped nuts, or herbs can enhance the flavor.

For cooking, use a clean, heated rock, a frying pan, or a green stick to cook over an open flame. If using a rock, heat it thoroughly over your fire and ensure it's clean. Place the dough on the surface or wrap it around the stick in a spiral. Cook the bread for 5-7 minutes on each side, or rotate the stick over the fire until the bread is golden brown and firm. Test doneness by tapping the bread—it should sound hollow. If the center is doughy, cook it a bit longer.

Bannock bread is best enjoyed warm and wild herbs, berries, or nuts can enhance your cooking and create unique flavors. If you're near the ocean, you can even boil seawater to collect salt as a seasoning.

Tips:

- Test the heat of your cooking surface by sprinkling water on it; if it sizzles gently, it's ready.

- If your dough feels sticky, dust it with extra flour.

- Cook small portions to ensure even cooking and avoid burning the outside.

With a little effort and creativity, you'll have a simple, delicious bread to complement your survival diet.

Flour from Versatile Ingredients

Flour isn't just a kitchen staple—it's a survival tool that connects us to our ancient ancestors. With a bit of effort and creativity, you can transform seeds, nuts, or roots into a versatile ingredient for baking, cooking, or even thickening stews. Here's how you can make flour from nature, even without modern tools.

The first step in making flour is choosing your base material; nature has plenty of options. Grains like wild wheat, barley, or oats are excellent choices in the right environment. If grains are scarce, look to wild grasses and their tiny seeds, or consider nuts like acorns, chestnuts, or hazelnuts. In wetter areas, dried roots from plants like cattails or arrowheads can also be ground into flour. Even legumes, like dried peas or beans, work. The key is to choose mature, clean, and abundant resources.

Preparation is key. After harvesting, spread your seeds, nuts, or roots in a sunny spot to dry completely. This prevents mold and makes grinding easier. If your material has a tough outer shell or husk, you'll need to remove it. Grains, for example, can be rubbed between your hands or lightly pounded with a stone to loosen the husks. Nuts will need a little more effort—cracking their shells with rocks or other hard surfaces is the best way to expose the edible insides.

When it's time to grind, find two flat, smooth stones. One will act as your grinding base, and the other as your grinder. Place your seeds or nuts on the base stone, then crush them with the upper stone using firm pressure and circular motions. This will gradually break the material into smaller particles.

Some materials need special handling. Acorns, for example, contain tannins that give them a bitter taste. To remove these, crush the acorns and soak them in water for several days, changing the water regularly. Once leached, dry them thoroughly and grind them into flour. Roots like cattails should be sliced thinly and dried entirely before grinding. For wild grasses, harvest the seeds and winnow them to remove the chaff before grinding.

Grinding flour without tools takes time and patience. Working in small batches can help keep things manageable. You can also get creative by mixing and matching different seeds or grains to make unique blends, adding variety to your diet.

Fire cooking isn't just about feeding your stomach; it's about feeding your soul. It's a way to connect with the elements, history, and each other. So next time you light up a fire, remember, you're not just making dinner but making memories. Grab your skewers, gather your logs, and let's turn up the heat on outdoor cooking!

Utilizing the Sun with a Solar Oven

Picture a solar cooker as your slow cooker's sun-powered cousin. These devices range from simple DIY setups involving reflective materials that focus sunlight onto a pot, to high-tech, commercially available models that can fry or steam your food. The magic happens best under clear skies with direct sunlight, ideally during midday when the sun is high. With no open flame, it allows you to leave your food unattended while it cooks; just avoid touching the heating surface because it gets ridiculously hot. This method isn't just about whipping up meals; it's a sustainable practice that reduces fuel consumption and keeps the air clean.

How to Make Your Own

There are countless designs and a quick internet search can boggle the brain with contraptions called 'Solar Ovens.' Here is a simple DIY setup. Be sure to expound upon this basic design for your personal cooking needs and what is readily available.

- **Prepare the Box**
  Find a cardboard box and create a lid similar to that of a pizza box being hinged to the base on one side.

- **Create the Reflector and Line the Interior**
  Cover the inside of the flap and line the inside of the box with aluminum foil, shiny side out. This helps retain and concentrate heat. Use glue, tape, or staples to secure the foil smoothly.

- **Add Black Paper**
  Cover the bottom of the box with black construction

paper, black trash bags, or dark colored pebbles. Black absorbs heat and helps the oven get hotter.

- **Set Up the Reflector**
Use a stick or ruler to prop open the foil-covered flap, angling it toward the sun. Adjust the angle to reflect the most sunlight into the box.

- **Position the Oven**
Place the solar oven in direct sunlight. Turn it occasionally to keep it aligned with the sun as it moves.

For those less inclined to build from scratch, the market is full of sleek designs that fold up for easy transport, perfect for your next camping trip or a more intense B.O.B. When choosing your solar oven, consider your local climate—consistent sunny weather calls for a basic model. At the same time, a more advanced setup with efficient heat retention might be better suited for areas with variable weather. Remember, the goal is to harness as much sunshine as possible, so pick a model that best fits your sunlit circumstances.

Cooking Tips and Recipes

Solar ovens excel at slow-cooked dishes. Think tender stews, succulent roasts, or your grandma's secret bean recipe. Start with something simple, like a hearty chili or baked sweet potatoes. Place your ingredients in a dark, thin-walled pot for maximum heat absorption, and let the sun work its magic. Patience is vital—solar cooking isn't a sprint; it's more of a leisurely stroll. On a bright, sunny day, expect your lunch to take a few hours to cook. But hey, it's worth the wait, and think of the energy you're saving! And here's a pro tip: preheat your solar oven for at least 30 minutes while prepping your ingredients to cut down on cooking time.

Egg Frittata

Gather 2-3 eggs and some foraged vegetables, such as wild greens, yams, onions, or mushrooms. Crack the eggs into a clean rock depression, aluminum foil, or another natural container. Use a clean stick or your fingers to whisk the eggs lightly, adding a pinch of salt and pepper if you have it. Chop or tear the vegetables into small pieces and mix them into the eggs. Find a flat, dark rock or a natural container that can act as your cooking dish, and coat it with a bit of animal fat or nut oil to prevent sticking. Pour the egg mixture into the dish and cover it with a large, flat leaf or other natural material to trap heat. Let it cook for 1-2 hours until the eggs are firm and cooked through.

Sun-Baked Fish

Freshwater fish such as trout, perch, and catfish are commonly found in streams and lakes. At the same time, saltwater varieties like mackerel and snapper are abundant in coastal regions. To prepare fish for cooking, start by scaling and gutting it thoroughly, removing all internal organs, and rinsing it clean. Season it generously with salt or seawater and sprinkle with wild herbs like thyme or rosemary. For added flavor, stuff the fish with additional herbs or a few lemon slices if available. Wrap the fish tightly in aluminum foil or place it on a dark, flat rock to maximize heat absorption. Place the fish in a solar oven and cook for 1.5-3 hours, adjusting the time based on the fish's size. It's ready when the flesh flakes easily with a fork, revealing a tender and flavorful meal.

Berry Cobbler

Forage about a cup of wild berries such as blueberries, raspberries, or blackberries. If you have sugar or honey, mix two tablespoons with the berries for sweetness and a squeeze of lemon, and then place in a small, dark container, like a hollowed-out piece of bark or a darkened stone bowl. For the topping, combine 1/4 cup of crushed nuts (hazelnuts, acorns, or other edible varieties) with one tablespoon of flour and two tablespoons of fat or oil (animal fat or foraged nut oil works well). Mix until crumbly, then sprinkle the mixture over the berries. Place the dish in your solar oven and let it cook for 1-2 hours or until the topping is golden and the berries are bubbling.

As you embark on the journey of solar cooking, you nourish your body with wholesome ingredients and feed your soul with the satisfaction of embracing sustainable living practices, knowing you can survive in the wild or during a crisis. Whether savoring your herb-infused fish on fresh bread or indulging in a berry cobbler, every bite celebrating the sun's generosity and the joy of crafting meals that resonate with flavor and intention.

Using Alternative Fuels

While solar and fire are stellar, exploring alternative fuels adds another layer to your off-grid culinary arsenal. Biomass briquettes, made from compressed organic waste like sawdust or leaves, provide a sustainable and efficient heat source. They burn cleaner than wood, reducing smoke and preserving your lungs while you cook. Then there are backpacking stoves, small and portable wonders that run on denatured alcohol, butane/ propane, or solid fuel tablets perfect for those less sunny days when solar cooking is off the menu. These stoves are great for boiling water or cooking small meals, making them a favorite among backpackers. Both options have their trade-offs; biomass briquettes require time to make or find, and alcohol stoves won't give you the high heat needed for certain dishes. However, incorporating these into your off-grid cooking practices ensures you're prepared, regardless of the weather or environment.

Preserving Foraged Foods

There's a special kind of satisfaction that comes from turning wild foraged plants, mushrooms, fish, or game into long-lasting provisions. Drying and smoking are two of the oldest and simplest preservation methods. With minimal equipment, you can ensure your wild bounty doesn't go to waste.

Principles of Drying and Dehydration

Why do we dehydrate food? Well, moisture is like a party invitation for bacteria and mold—remove it, and you drastically slow down their spoilage shenanigans. But it's not just about making food last longer; drying also concentrates the flavors, turning grapes into raisins and plums into prunes, each bursting with intensified sweetness and tang. You have a few methods to choose from: sun drying, air drying, and dehydrators. Sun drying is as simple as it sounds—slices of fruit or veggies laid out under the sun on a drying rack, a method used since ancient times. It's perfect for hot, dry climates where the sun is your reliable ally. Air drying works well for herbs—just hang bunches in a warm, well-ventilated area and let nature do the rest. For the gadget lovers, dehydrators are your go-to. These handy machines use low temperatures and fans to strip moisture, ensuring even drying without cooking the food. The result? You get to enjoy summer's bounty all year round, and your trail mix will never be bland again.

How to Utilize the Air

Ready to try your hand at these techniques?

- Gather Materials: Collect a few wooden frames, which you can make from scrap wood, purchase inexpensively, or repurpose from an old window frame. You'll also need food-safe mesh, a staple gun, and twine or wire for hanging.

- Prepare the Frames: If you're making your own frames, cut the wood to your desired size (approximately 2 feet by 2 feet is ideal) and assemble them using nails or screws to ensure they are sturdy.

- Attach the Mesh: Cut the mesh to fit each frame, then securely attach using the staple gun or twine if necessary. Keep the mesh pulled tight to create a flat surface.

- Create Air Circulation: If you plan to stack multiple frames, use small wooden blocks or dowels to create space between each layer. Attach these spacers to the corners of the frames to ensure proper air circulation.

- Set Up the Rack: To maximize drying efficiency, hang your drying rack in a well-ventilated, dry area or place it on a sunny surface with good airflow.

Herbs can be spread in a single layer and typically dry within a few days. Thinly sliced apples laid out on the mesh without overlapping will take several days to a week to dry, depending on the humidity. This simple project helps you preserve the flavors and benefits of your harvest year-round. Place it in a sunny spot, or if you're using it indoors, ensure it's in a dry, warm area with good air circulation.

Smoking and Curing Meats

Let's talk about turning your backyard into a smokehouse and your kitchen table into a charcuterie board. Smoking and curing meats are not just ways to wow your foodie friends or prep for the apocalypse; they're ancient methods that have jazzed up the human diet for centuries. So why do we smoke and cure meats? Well, apart from making things deliciously interesting, these methods are fantastic for extending the shelf life.

Introduction to Curing and Smoking

Back in the day, before refrigerators were a glint in electricity's eye, smoking and curing were the go-to methods for preserving meats. The magic lies in the slow, gentle application of smoke and the careful use of salts, which not only keep the harmful microorganisms at bay but also infuse the meat with flavors that'll make your taste buds sing. Curing can bring out a savory depth that's hard to resist, while smoking imparts a rich, woodsy flavor. These methods aren't just about preservation; they enhance flavor, making each bite a testament to your culinary prowess.

Basics of Curing Meats

Think of it as giving your meats a spa treatment with salt, sugar, and spices. This process begins with selecting the appropriate type of meat, commonly pork (for bacon and ham), beef (for corned beef and pastrami), or fish. The meat is then covered with a mixture of salt and curing agents, often called curing salt or pink salt, which contains sodium nitrite or sodium nitrate. This mixture can also include sugar, which adds flavor and helps balance the saltiness. Herbs and spices like bay leaves, peppercorns, and juniper berries can be added for additional flavor.

There are two primary methods of curing: dry curing and wet curing (brining). In dry curing, the meat is coated with the dry cure mixture and left to cure in a cool, dry place for a specified period, typically several days to a few weeks. This method is often used for products like prosciutto and pancetta. Wet curing involves submerging the meat in a brine solution made with 1 cup of salt per gallon of water and curing agents. This method is commonly used for corned beef and some types of bacon. The curing time varies depending on the size and type of meat, ranging from a few days to several weeks.

After the curing period, the meat is rinsed to remove excess salt and dried. At this stage, some meats are ready to be cooked or smoked. In contrast, others, like certain hams and salamis, may undergo additional aging to develop more complex flavors. Properly cured meat can be stored in the refrigerator for extended periods. In some cases, like cured hams, it can be stored at room temperature if kept in a cool, dry place. The key to successful curing is maintaining cleanliness, consistent temperatures, and precise measurements of curing agents to ensure safety and quality. The key is balance, whether you're prepping bacon, curing hams, or making jerky; too little salt won't preserve properly, and too much can turn dinner into a salt lick. Experiment with flavors by mixing herbs, garlic, or whatever tickles your fancy to create a signature cure that's all your own.

Tools and Techniques for Smoking Meats

Smoking is one of the oldest methods of food preservation, utilized by cultures worldwide to extend the shelf life of perishable items while imparting a unique flavor. Smoking works by drying out the food and infusing it with smoke compounds that have antimicrobial properties. Key components that contribute to preservation include heat, which reduces moisture content; smoke containing chemicals like phenols and formaldehyde that act as preservatives; and salt, which is often used in conjunction with smoking to draw out moisture and add a layer of preservation. You can use a fancy electric smoker with all the bells and whistles or keep it rustic with a drum smoker made from an old metal barrel. Each type has its charm and accomplishes the same purpose, but the key is consistent low heat and good smoke flow.

Popular meats include beef, pork, poultry, and game meat. The process typically involves brining or dry curing to season and preserve the meat. After curing, rinse the meat or fish with fresh water, pat dry, and let air dry until a pellicle forms—a sticky surface that helps the smoke to adhere better. Smoking can be done through cold smoking, performed at temperatures below 85°F for flavoring without cooking, or hot smoking, done at temperatures between 225°F to 250°F to cook and smoke the meat simultaneously. Properly smoked meat can be stored in the refrigerator for a few weeks or frozen for longer preservation.

Fish, particularly fatty varieties like salmon, trout, mackerel, and herring, are ideal for smoking. The preparation involves brining and drying to form a pellicle, followed by either cold smoking for delicate fish or hot smoking to cook and smoke the fish.

Health and Safety Tips

Before you set out to smoke or cure the next great snack, a word on safety: keeping things clean is crucial. Always start with fresh, high-quality meats, and keep your tools and workspace sanitized. Monitor temperatures closely when smoking to ensure even cooking, and always cure meats in a cool, dry place.

Conclusion

Preparing your finds in the wild using an open flame, smoking, and solar techniques is more than just making food; it's about connecting with nature and honoring ancient traditions. Each method brings unique flavors and textures, turning your meals into culinary adventures. These practices foster a deeper appreciation for the natural world, promote sustainability, and provide a fulfilling way to nourish body and soul.

CHAPTER EIGHT

TOOLS, TRAPS AND TRACKING TECHNIQUES

I n this chapter, we will embark on a journey into handcrafted mechanisms and tools, both big and small. Get ready to test those observation skills, as we will meticulously note the various footprints, scat, and signs left behind by wildlife, allowing us better to understand their behavior and movements through the environment. Whether you're a seasoned trapper or someone who thinks 'game' is just something you play on your phone, this chapter will equip you with the know-how to interact with nature responsibly and sustainably.

Handcrafting Basic Tools

First things first, let's talk design. Crafting practical tools starts with a plan. What do you need? A knife for cutting? A hook for fishing? Start with the end in mind. Your design doesn't need to be worthy of a Da Vinci sketch but should address the functionality: size, shape, and the forces it will need to withstand. For Materials, nature's bounty is rich—wood, stone, bone, and more are all up for grabs. Each material has its quirks. Wood is versatile and easy to carve but can lack the durability for heavy-duty tasks. Stone is tough and great for cutting edges or pounding tools but shaping it can be a workout. Bone, often overlooked, is fantastic for finer tools like needles or fishhooks.

Imagine you're a chef in a wild pantry: selecting the right ingredient for your dish is crucial. Similarly, choosing the suitable material for your tool ensures its effectiveness and longevity. For instance, hardwood like oak or maple is perfect for a sturdy knife handle. At the same time, a harder stone like flint or obsidian is ideal for a sharp, durable blade. The key is to match the material's properties with the tool's intended use, ensuring that it won't just perform well but will also stand the test of time (and survival).

Carving and Shaping a Spoon

Transforming a raw piece of wood or bone into a functional tool is immensely satisfying. Let's say you're making a spoon from a piece of hardwood. Start by sketching the rough shape of the spoon on the wood. Using a sharp knife or a piece of flint, begin to carve out the basic shape. If you're working with wood, follow the grain to avoid splitting. A curved blade works best for hollowing out the spoon's bowl, but a lump of hot coal can burn out the hollow in a pinch, then smoothed with a smaller tool. Sanding down the edges with a rough stone or abrasive leaves can give your spoon that finished feel. It's a process of patience and attention to detail, turning a simple block of wood into a functional piece of art.

Making a Multi-Purpose Knife

Let's keep putting theory into action by crafting a basic survival knife. Begin by finding a suitable piece of hard stone like flint or obsidian for the blade and a sturdy piece of wood or bone for the handle. With patience and careful attention, shape the blade by knapping (to strike, shape, or work) away at the stone, focusing on creating a sharp edge while taking precautions like using protective gear to shield against sharp fragments. As you shape the handle, consider its design, ensuring it provides a secure grip and can withstand the rigors of survival tasks. Attach the blade to the handle using natural adhesives such as pine resin or plant sap and reinforce the connection with bindings made from strips of leather or plant fibers for added strength.

Cooking Implements

For creativity in the kitchen, start by gathering clay-rich soil near water sources. Clean and knead the clay thoroughly to remove debris, achieving a smooth texture. Shape by pinching and smoothing the clay into a bowl shape, gradually building the walls to an even thickness. Flatten the bottom for stability and smooth the inside and outside surfaces with your hands or a stone. Allow the pot to air dry in a shaded area for several days, ensuring it dries evenly to avoid cracking. Optionally, fire the dried pot in a bonfire or pit kiln to harden it further. Once cooled, the finished pot can be optionally sealed with natural substances like beeswax or pine resin. This process produces functional vessels for cooking or storage but also honors the timeless craft of pottery-making through simple, hands-on techniques.

Maintenance and Care of Natural Tools

Finally, let's talk about care and maintenance. Natural tools, while effective, require a bit more TLC to keep them in working order. Regular cleaning is crucial, especially for tools used in food preparation or regularly exposed to moisture. A scrub with sand and quick rinse can remove dirt and grime. Sharpening your tools is also essential; a dull tool is a dangerous tool. A piece of harder stone or even a smooth ceramic shard can sharpen edges. Storing your tools in a dry, sheltered place ensures they are protected from the elements and ready for use when you need them next. It's about respecting the resources you've used, ensuring their longevity and effectiveness for as long as you need them.

Fishing Poles, Hooks, and Entanglements

This section is not solely focused on catching fish; it's about immersing yourself in the ancient skills of self-reliance, embracing the simplicity of nature, and experiencing the satisfaction of creating something functional with your own hands. So, let's untangle the basics of creating a way to catch dinner or just pass an afternoon telling stories about "the one that got away."

Making a Fishing Pole

To construct such, one must...

1. **Find the Perfect Stick:**

   ○ Look for a long, straight, and flexible branch or sapling, ideally around 6-8 feet long. Green wood is your best bet as it's more flexible and less likely to snap.

   ○ Remove any leaves, branches, or twigs. You can do this with your hands or by rubbing the stick against a rough surface like a rock. The goal is to create a smooth, straight pole that's easy to handle.

2. **Prepare the Cordage:**

   ○ Use natural fibers such as long grasses or strips of bark for cordage. If you have shoelaces or any string, that's even better.

   ○ Ensure your cordage is long enough to reach the water and has some extra length for casting.

- Secure one end of the line to the thinner end of your stick, ensuring it's tight and secure. This is your line, so it needs to hold up under pressure.

3. Make the Hook:

- Find a small, strong piece of bone, a large thorn, or a sturdy stick.

- If using bone or thorn, sharpen one end to form a point and create a small notch or groove near the other end to tie the line.

- If using wood, sharpen one end to a point and carefully bend it into a hook shape by heating the wood over a fire to make it more pliable. Carve a small notch near the top.

- Attach this hook to the end of your cordage with another secure knot, ensuring it is sharp and sturdy enough to withstand a fish's struggle.

4. Prepare the Bait:

- Look around for worms, insects, or small pieces of food that can be used as bait.

- Attach the bait to your hook.

5. Fishing:

- Cast your line into the water.

- Patience is a virtue and remember, some people do this just for fun!

Understanding Fish Trap Mechanics

The principles behind fish traps are simple yet remarkably effective. They utilize passive capture techniques that allow fish to swim into a contained space they cannot escape from.

There are several types of fish traps to consider, each suited to different environments and target species. Basket traps, for instance are often used in stationary, calm waters. They might look like submerged baskets with funnel-shaped openings that welcome fish but confuse them when they try to leave. Funnel traps work on a similar principle but are typically narrower and longer, which makes them ideal for streams or rivers where their shape can channel fish straight into the trap. Then, there are larger and more complex corral traps, which can encompass areas in tidal waters where fish tend to gather, guiding them into an enclosed space.

Materials for Making Fish Traps

You'll need sturdy materials that can withstand water currents and the thrashing of captured fish while being gentle on the environment. Bamboo is a top choice for many DIY trap builders due to its strength, flexibility, and sustainability. It can be cut and shaped into frames for basket or funnel traps or used whole for structural supports in corral traps. Vines or flexible branches can be woven into the gaps to create a mesh that lets water flow but keeps fish in. Even recycled plastic bottles or old wire mesh can be transformed into efficient funnel traps, where the fish easily swim into the trap but not back out.

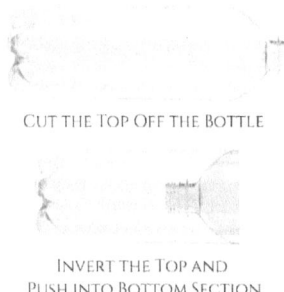

CUT THE TOP OFF THE BOTTLE

INVERT THE TOP AND
PUSH INTO BOTTOM SECTION

The Inverted Bottle

You'll need a large plastic bottle (2 liters or larger), a sharp knife or scissors, and some string:

Cut off the top third of the bottle and insert it back into the bottom to form a funnel. Secure this funnel in place with string, ensuring it fits tightly.

Make a few small holes around the neck and along the sides of the inverted top to allow water flow.

Once assembled, bait the trap with something appealing to fish, such as breadcrumbs or small insects, and place it in the water with the opening facing downstream. Fish will swim in through the funnel and become trapped inside.

Stone Sculpting

To construct a stone fish trap, you'll need stones of various sizes and a shallow, narrow stream or river:

1. Find a shallow, narrow section of a stream or river.

2. Arrange the stones in a V-shaped formation, with the point of the V facing downstream. The sides should extend towards the banks.

3. At the point of the V, create a corral or holding area where fish can be trapped.

4. Ensure the structure is sturdy and the gaps between the stones are minimal.

As fish swim downstream, they will be funneled into the narrow point of the V and trapped in the corral. This method is simple to execute, requires no specialized tools, and effectively utilizes the natural landscape to catch fish.

Best Practices for Trap Placement and Maintenance

Choosing the right spot to place your trap is as crucial as building it properly. Look for areas where fish are known to congregate, such as near submerged logs, weed beds, or underwater structures. The water depth, current, and the behavior of the target fish species should guide your placement. For example, a stone trap in a flowing stream might best be placed near the edge where it's shallow enough to build your walls. At the same time, a funnel trap in a river might need a secure spot where the current is steady but not too swift.

Regularly maintaining your trap is crucial to ensuring it remains effective and humane. Check it frequently to remove captured fish and clear any debris or damage. This prevents the fish from suffering unnecessarily and maintains the trap's structure and functionality.

Safety and Environmental Considerations

Fishing, like any outdoor activity, comes with its responsibilities. Handling your gear safely, particularly hooks, is paramount. Always be mindful of where your hooks are for your safety and that of others. When dealing with caught fish, handle them with respect. If you plan to release a fish, do so gently, ensuring it's strong enough to swim away. Adhering to local fishing regulations keeps you on the right side of the law, contributing to sustainable fishing practices and ensuring that future generations can enjoy the same thrill of the catch. So grab that line and prepare for a tug-of-war with nature, where every catch is a story, and every outing is an adventure.

Snares and Traps for Small Game

When it comes to living off the grid, or just infusing a bit of wilderness into our over-civilized lives, the skill of trapping can make you feel like a real frontiersman (or woman!). But before you go setting traps willy-nilly, it's crucial to tune in to the behaviors of the wildlife around you. Understanding animal behavior isn't just about making successful captures; it's about interacting with nature in a respectful and sustainable way. For instance, knowing that rabbits often follow the same paths—called runs—can help you place snares effectively without causing undue stress to the animal population. It's about being a thoughtful participant in the natural world, not just a bystander.

Cage Traps

When you think of traps, you might envision something out of an old cartoon—maybe a box propped up with a stick, waiting for an unsuspecting critter to wander in. Well, you're not too far off, cage traps, are indeed a real and effective method for capturing small game, especially if you're looking for a non-lethal option. Building a box trap can be a delightful weekend project using materials you might already have lying around. Start with a sturdy box or wire cage large enough for your target animal. You can repurpose household items like a fishing line, a wooden dowel, and some basic hardware for the trigger and door mechanism. The key is ensuring the mechanism is sensitive enough to close swiftly when triggered but sturdy enough to hold securely once shut.

1. Find an area frequented by the target animal, ideally near visible signs of their activity.

2. Choose a sturdy wooden or cardboard box large enough to contain the once-trapped animal.

3. Find a stick or dowel about 12-18 inches long to prop up the box.

4. Tie one end of the string to the prop stick. The other end will pull the stick away and close the trap.

5. Prop up one end of the box with the stick, creating an open space for the animal to enter. The box should be tilted just enough to fall when the stick is removed.

6. Place the bait inside the box, positioning it near the back to ensure the animal is fully inside when reaching for it. Depending on the target animal, suitable baits include fruits, vegetables, or nuts.

7. Extend the string from the prop stick to a hidden spot where you can observe the trap without being seen. Ensure the string is long enough to reach your hiding spot.

8. Wait for the animal to enter the box. When it does, pull the string to remove the prop stick, causing the box to fall and trap the animal inside.

This method is simple and effective for catching small animals, providing a humane way to capture them for relocation or study.

Loop Snare

There are countless methods to set a snare, each tailored to different animals and perhaps even more than imagined! A quick Google search yields hundreds of thousands of results, leading to videos, infographics, and guides on setting snares. Some snares use a bent sapling tree as a trigger; when sprung, the tree tightens the noose and lifts the animal off the ground. Others are simpler, consisting of a loop placed over a game trail with small sticks and branches on either side to guide the animal into the snare.

The key to setting a snare correctly is ensuring it will close and hold the animal when it passes through. Each environment, game trail, and burrow is unique, requiring creativity for successful snare setting. It's important to remember there is no single correct way to set a snare trap, as long as it effectively captures the animal.

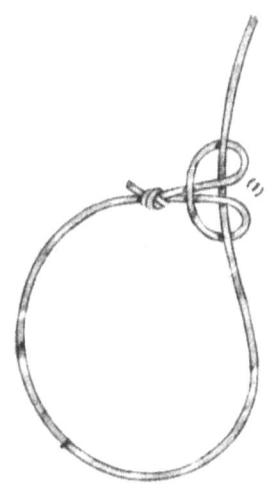

One of the simplest to construct is a basic slip knot attached to a tree. The loop can be held in place by a couple of small sticks at the approximate head height of the animal you aim to catch. Placing this snare along the animal's trail increases your chances of success. Almost any type of string can be used, with paracord being an excellent choice, though even a shoelace can work in a pinch.

Optionally, you can place bait inside the noose loop to attract the animal's attention and encourage it to enter the trap. While not always necessary, especially if you're putting your snare on a busy trail, the correct bait can significantly increase your chances of success. The key is using bait that is irresistible to the local wildlife, whether fresh berries, grains, or a dab of peanut butter. Be mindful of scent contamination—animals are incredibly attuned to human smells. Wearing gloves and boots that minimize scent can make trapping efforts more effective.

Ethics and Legality

Each region has its rules governing wildlife trapping, and for good reason. These laws help maintain animal populations and ensure that ecosystems remain balanced. Before setting out any trap, make sure you're familiar with local regulations—this can include specific seasons for trapping certain animals, licenses required, and restrictions on the types of traps used. Ethics go beyond legality, though. They touch on our respect and responsibility towards other creatures that share our planet, such as checking your traps regularly to avoid leaving an animal in distress and using the most humane dispatch methods available. Always aim to use your skills to support sustainable practices that ensure wildlife populations remain healthy for generations to come.

As you delve into the trapping world, you'll find it's as much about understanding the environment and its inhabitants as it is about the traps' mechanics. Each successful capture is a testament to your skills and respect for the natural world, and each release is a reminder of the delicate balance we maintain as partisans of both conservation and consumption.

Bows, Arrows, and Fundamentals

Ah, the noble bow. It is not just a weapon of ancient warriors and mythical heroes but also a tool connecting us to the essence of survival and skill. Understanding how to craft and master a bow can add an invaluable layer to your survival toolkit.

Selecting Materials for Bow Making

You want solid yet flexible wood, capable of handling the immense stress of bending under tension without snapping. Woods such as yew, ash, and hickory are the A-listers in traditional bow-making circles, celebrated for their perfect blend of strength and elasticity. Each type of wood has its own character and grain patterns, which influence the bow's performance and durability. Bamboo, too, can be a fantastic choice, especially for those looking for a more sustainable material. It's remarkably strong and has a natural flexibility, making it an excellent choice.

Crafting Your Bow

Creating a basic longbow is like sculpting; you start with a rough outline and gradually refine it into something beautiful and functional. You'll need a strong, flexible piece of wood, a knife or sharp stone, and durable cordage:

1. Find a sturdy, flexible piece of wood about 5-6 feet long and 1-2 inches in diameter.

2. Using a knife or sharp stone, carve the wood to taper it towards the ends, leaving the middle section thicker for strength. Aim for a D-shaped cross-section.

3. Cut small notches near both ends of the wood to hold the bowstring. Ensure the notches are deep enough to secure the string but not so deep that they weaken the wood.

4. Find durable cordage, such as natural fibers (sinew, plant fibers) or synthetic material if available. The string should be slightly shorter than the bow to provide the necessary tension.

5. Secure one end of the string in a notch, then bend the bow to attach the other end in the opposite notch. The bow should have a gentle curve when strung.

6. Ensure the string is taut but not overly tight. Adjust as needed by tightening or loosening the knots at the notches.

7. Draw the string back gradually to test the bow's flexibility and strength. Make sure it bends evenly and returns to its original shape.

Crafting Your Arrows

To construct arrows in the wild, you'll need straight, sturdy sticks, feathers, sharp stones or metal shards, and natural cordage:

1. Find straight, sturdy sticks about 2-3 feet long and roughly 1/4 inch in diameter. Willow, dogwood, or birch are good choices.

2. If the sticks are slightly crooked, gently heat them over a fire and bend them. Hold them straight until they cool.

3. Use a knife or sharp stone to carve one end of each stick to a point. Put a V notch at the end of the stick and attach your small sharp stones or metal shards using natural cordage or resin for added durability and accuracy.

4. Carve a small notch at the other end of each stick to hold the bowstring. The notch should be deep enough to secure the string but not so deep that it weakens the arrow.

5. Collect feathers and split them in half. You'll need three feathers per arrow for optimal stability.

6. Using natural cordage or sinew, attach the feathers around the notched end of the arrow in a triangular formation. Secure the feathers tightly to ensure they stay in place.

7. Hold the arrows horizontally on your finger to ensure they are well-balanced. Adjust the fletching or point if necessary to achieve a proper balance.

These handmade arrows, when paired with your bow, will provide you with functional projectiles for hunting or practice.

Fundamentals of Archery

With your bow crafted, it's time to master the art of marksmanship. Archery is more than just shooting arrows; it's about posture, precision, and patience. Your stance is the foundation—feet shoulder-width apart, body perpendicular to the target, and a stable base like the roots of a tree. Gripping the bow is next; hold it firmly but not too tightly, like a handshake. When drawing the bow, it's all in the arms and shoulders, pulling back smoothly until the hand is under the jaw, the string lightly touching the side of your nose. Aiming, breathe out slowly, find your target, and release. The consistency of this process is what builds accuracy over time. Practice, as they say, makes perfect.

Hunting with a Bow

Bowhunting is a dance between hunter and hunted, a practice that demands skill with the weapon and an understanding of the animal you're pursuing. Tracking, stalking, and knowing where to aim are as crucial as the shot. Always aim for a clean, humane kill; this means understanding animal anatomy and shooting at the vital organs. Ensure you're familiar with local regulations, have the necessary permits, and always respect the wildlife and their habitat. Whether for sport, survival, or simply for the joy of learning an ancient art, archery can enrich your life, providing protection and a profound sense of connection to the past and the natural world around you.

Tracking and Observations

Animal tracking is about noticing and understanding the marks animals leave as they move about their environment. These can range from footprints (tracks) to droppings (scat) to signs of feeding or bedding down. Each mark tells a story, and learning to read these signs can give you insights into the animal's size, diet, state of health, and even its intentions. For instance, the depth and clarity of a deer's hoof prints can tell you how fast

Deer

it was moving and how recently it passed by. Similarly, the presence of scat can reveal what the animal has been eating, which can help you understand where it might be headed next.

The Prime Location

Observing animals in their natural habitat can teach you about timing and placement for your traps. Deer, for example, are crepuscular, meaning they're most active during dawn and dusk. Setting up near feeding areas during these times can increase your chances of a successful catch.

Turkey

Similarly, understanding that squirrels are likely to scavenge near fallen trees—where nuts and fruits are abundant—can guide you to set up traps in these prime spots. This kind of knowledge doesn't just make trapping easier; it makes it more humane and reduces the time animals might spend in distress.

Rabbit

Conclusion

As we near the end of our exploration, I can't help but feel a deep sense of accomplishment and connection to the ancient traditions we've explored. We've learned how to carve a simple yet functional spoon from a piece of wood and transform raw materials into a fishing pole from scratch. Making snares teaches us the delicate balance of patience and precision required to capture game, while constructing a bow and arrow brings us closer to the resourcefulness and ingenuity of our ancestors. Each of these projects equips us with practical survival skills and reminds us of the beauty and simplicity of nature's offerings.

RESILIENT REFLECTIONS

From those first tentative steps of packing your BOB to mastering the fine arts of foraging and fermenting, you've journeyed far from the shores of uncertainty to the rugged cliffs of self-sufficiency. Remember when we started? The idea was not to get overwhelmed by a blackout or a snowed-in weekend. Now look at us—ready to tackle just about anything Mother Nature whimsically tosses our way!

Throughout this book, we've covered a lot of ground. From mastering the art of constructing sturdy shelters, harnessing solar ovens, and honing critical survival skills like fire-making, water-finding, foraging, toolmaking, and emergency preparedness. We embrace not just practicality but a deeper connection to our ancestral heritage. Each skill learned, from crafting fishhooks that echo ancient wisdom to using salt and sugar to preserve a future snack, reinforces our resilience and respect for nature's gifts.

The recent fire in my life sparked a profound realization of the importance of preparedness. In outdoor survival, preparation is not just a prudent choice but a lifeline that separates adventure from adversity, turning panic into purpose. Reflecting on my experiences, whether navigating by the stars or predicting weather changes, each lesson learned contributes significantly to a sense of empowerment and readiness. Every knot tied and spoon carved serves as a building block toward self-sufficiency and resilience in the face of nature's unpredictability

For those hungry to continue learning, the landscape of resources is vast and ever-expanding. Online platforms offer a wealth of knowledge through specialized websites, comprehensive courses, and interactive forums where seasoned experts and fellow enthusiasts share insights and strategies. These digital trails provide a gateway to deepen your understanding of survival techniques. Each resource opens doors to new perspectives, techniques, and community interactions, fostering a learning environment that encourages exploration and skill development at your own pace. Whether you're refining your outdoor survival toolkit or delving into advanced wilderness first aid, these resources ensure that the journey of learning is as enriching and dynamic as the wild itself.

As we come to the end of this chapter, both in the literal sense of our discussions and metaphorically in our journey of preparation, it's crucial to recognize that the world around us constantly evolves. Yet, armed with the skills and knowledge acquired, you're not merely prepared to endure but to excel. With a courageous heart and a readiness to face any storm, no challenge will be impossible. Embrace the future confidently, knowing that every obstacle is an opportunity for growth and that every step forward is a chance to shape a brighter tomorrow. Here's to embracing knowledge, courage, and community—qualities that empower us to adapt and thrive in a rapidly evolving environment.

As we embark on this journey of discovery and mastery, we honor the legacy of those who came before us and ensure that these invaluable skills endure for generations.

KEEPING THE ADVENTURE ALIVE

Now you have the confidence needed to survive and thrive in the great outdoors, it's time to pass on your newfound knowledge and show other readers where they can find this knowledge crafted by nature!

Simply by leaving your honest opinion of this book on Amazon, you'll show others interested in learning survival techniques where they can find the information to learn these invaluable skills too.

Thank you for your help. The spirit of adventure and self-reliance is kept alive when we pass on our knowledge – and you're helping me to do just that.

Aloha,

Kapena Marina

INVESTIGATIONS INTO THE INTER WEB

References

- *Make A Plan* https://www.ready.gov/plan

- *How to Build a Home Resistant to Natural Disasters* ... https://www.gjgardner.com/planning-your-build/how-to-build-a-home-thats-resistant-to-natural-disasters/

- *Essential Foraging Tools and Supplies* ... https://chestnutherbs.com/essential-foraging-tools-and-supplies/

- *Create Your Family Emergency Communication Plan* ... https://www.ready.gov/sites/default/files/2020-03/family-emergency-communication-planning-document.pdf

- *Get in Formation: A Community Safety Toolkit* ... https://visionchangewin.org/wp-content/uploads/2020/07/VCW-Safety-Toolkit-R2.pdf

- *A beginner's guide to finding wild edible plants that won't* ... https://www.popsci.com/find-wild-edible-plants/

- *Foraging Wild Edibles: Dietary Diversity in Expanded Food* ... https://www.ncbi.nlm.nih.gov/pmc/articles/PMC10647252/

- *Preserving Wild Food: Drying or Blanching / Freezing Edible* ... https://www.ediblewildfood.com/preserving-food.aspx

- *Methods To Cook Off-Grid Without Power - Survival Mom* ... https://thesurvivalmom.com/off-grid-cooking-methods/

- *Automated plant species identification—Trends and future* ... https://www.ncbi.nlm.nih.gov/pmc/articles/PMC5886388/

- *7 Surprising Health Benefits of Eating Seaweed - Healthline* ... https://www.healthline.com/nutrition/benefits-of-seaweed

- *A Foraging Guide for All of the 50 US States* ... https://discover.texasrealfood.com/foraging/foraging-guide-for-all-50-us-states

- *Open AI 2024 Chat GPT4O* ... https://chatgpt.com/

Would also like to include a reference to my mother's wisdom! I have relied on her knowledge and skills passed down and as an anchor while writing this book. She's better than any search engine... Love & Appreciate you Mom, Mahalo Nui Loa!